Jean Bodin and the Rise of Absolutist Theory

JULIAN H. FRANKLIN

Professor of Government, Columbia University

CAMBRIDGE

at the University Press

1973

Published by the Syndics of the Cambridge University Press
Bentley House, 200 Euston Road, London NW1 2DB
American Branch: 32 East 57th Street, New York, N.Y. 10022

© Cambridge University Press 1973

Library of Congress Catalogue Card Number: 72 83666

ISBN: 0 521 20000 8

Typeset by The Eastern Press Ltd. of London and Reading
Printed in the United States of America

Contents

For Paula

Preface

One consequence of the St Bartholomew's Day Massacre of 1572 was the polarization of French constitutional ideas. Appearing on the one side was a radicalized version of the French constitution, which was advanced by the Huguenots to justify resistance. On the other side, and in opposition to it, was the theory of royal absolutism systematically developed by Bodin.

The central thesis of this book is that Bodin's absolutism was as unprecedented as the doctrine it opposed. Prior to the 1570s the mainstream of the French tradition had been tentatively constitutionalist, and Bodin himself had given strong expression to that tendency in his *Methodus* of 1566. His earlier theory of sovereignty, elaborated in that work, was implicitly adapted to a notion of limited supremacy.

Ten years later, with the publication of his *République*, this position was abandoned. But the absolutism of the later work was so confused and strained that it cannot be taken as the natural outcome of the older view. It was rather an abrupt, and largely ill-founded, departure not only in Bodin's intellectual career but in the general movement of French and European thought. It cannot be fully understood except as an ideological reaction to the seeming menace of the newer constitutionalism.

In the present work I have tried to explain how this absolutist view was formed. Insofar as I have been successful, I shall also have clarified at least some of the obscurities for which Bodin's thought has been notorious. I should like to think that this study will also be of use to students of a later period. Much absolutist doctrine of the seventeenth century was either based on Bodin's theory or else relied on similar assumptions.

All translations are my own unless otherwise indicated. All quotations have been translated in the notes as well as in the text.

All citations to the French version of the *République* refer to the Scientia Verlag facsimile reprint of the 1583 edition (Aalen, Germany, 1961), and all citations to the *Methodus* refer to the text of the edition of 1572 edited (with a French translation) by Pierre Mesnard (Presses Universitaires, Paris, 1951). Citations to these works also include references, in parentheses, to corresponding passages in the English translations. For the *République*, the numbers in parentheses refer to the facsimile reprint of the Knolles translation of 1606, edited and introduced by Kenneth D. McRae (Harvard, 1962). For the *Methodus* they refer to the translation by Beatrice Reynolds (Columbia, 1945).

In many citations two dates are given. The former refers either to the first edition, to the main edition in the author's lifetime, or in some cases to the date when the work was composed. I have done this only for works written or published in or about the sixteenth century, and only where the date of the edition actually used is different. The additional date has been given only in the initial citation of a work.

I should like to thank the many friends and colleagues who gave me help and encouragement. My fellow-members of the University Seminar for the Study of Political and Social Thought at Columbia University discussed parts of an earlier version of this book in manuscript. At various times I benefited from conversations and exchanges with Ralph E. Giesey of the University of Iowa, John H. M. Salmon of Bryn Mawr College, and especially Donald R. Kelley of the New York State University at Binghamton, who was very often a source of helpful information and stimulating criticism. In preparing the present version I was very much indebted to Abraham Ascher of Brooklyn College for his thoughtful encouragement and to William L. Weinstein of Oxford University for a very useful conversation on the concept of limited supremacy. I am grateful to Donald R. Kelley and to Herbert A. Deane of Columbia University for careful readings of the final typescript.

I should like to thank the Council for Research in the Social Sciences of Columbia University and the European Institute of Columbia University for grants in aid of my research during the academic year 1968-9. The European Institute was then directed by the late Philip E. Mosely whose generosity to students as well as colleagues is already becoming a legend at Columbia. I also profited greatly from my attendance at the Internationale Bodin Tagung, Munich, 1970, which was organized by the Geschwister-Scholl-Institut für politische Wissenschaft of the University of Munich. The papers delivered at the Conference, together with reports of the discussions and a comprehensive Bodin bibliography, will soon be published.

I am, finally, especially grateful to my wife, Paula, not only for her editorial assistance but for her patience and encouragement throughout.

J.H.F.

New York City
February 1972

CHAPTER 1

The Persistence of Medieval Constitutionalism

Absolutism as a coherent body of political thought appeared rather late in France, and considerably later than was once supposed.[1] With the growth of ' centralized ' monarchies in the late Middle Ages and the Renaissance, the medieval tradition of consent was refocused rather than erased, and in some respects was actually strengthened. If the king's subjection of feudal magnates and corporate communities had tended to weaken the traditional checks, the new administrative and consultative institutions served as new limits upon royal power, even though they were nominally created by the kings themselves. The traditional idea of limitations thus persisted in an altered form and even continued to develop through most of the sixteenth century.

The character of this development is not always easy to detect. Constitutionalist ideas are often overlaid by an absolutist rhetoric that is not always seriously intended. Since the ideas themselves are cautious and at times ambiguous, they are easily eclipsed by the bolder and rather different constitutionalism that appeared abruptly after the St Bartholomew's Day Massacre of 1572. Nevertheless, the constitutionalist motifs of roughly the century preceding St Bartholomew's have a shape and direction of their own which it is the purpose of this chapter to describe. For there seems to be no better way to arrive at a clear understanding and precise evaluation of the absolutist theory that was introduced with Jean Bodin's *Six livres de la république*.[2]

---

[1] For the view that absolutism predominated in the sixteenth century, see, for example, Pierre Mesnard, *L'essor de la philosophie politique au XVIe siècle*, 2nd ed. (Paris, 1951) p. 490, and also J. W. Allen, *Political Thought in the Sixteenth Century* (London, 1928) (1957) p. 283. More accurate in my opinion is William F. Church, *Constitutional Thought in Sixteenth-Century France* (Cambridge, Mass., 1941) pp. 74ff, which is indispensable for understanding French constitutional doctrine in this period.

[2] Roland Mousnier and Fritz Hartung do not stress this sort of ideological change in their ' Quelques problèmes concernant la monarchie absolue ', *Relazioni del X congresso internazionale di scienze storiche* (Florence, 1955) IV, *Storia moderna*, pp. 3–55. ' This notion of absolutism oscillates, as it were, around a point of equilibrium between a less and more limited conception of power. Depending on the circumstances, the personality of the sovereign and his ministers, the international situation, the movement of social classes, and economic contingencies, one or the other of these nuances of absolutism assumes more importance, without there being, overall, any serious changes in the notion itself.' On a less global perspective there would seem to be a very important change in ideology in the last quarter of the sixteenth century in France, and something of this is indicated, *ibid.* p. 11. But for Mousnier and Hartung the difference between the consultative and absolutist

Centralization of the monarchy in France had begun fairly early in the Middle Ages with the efforts of the Capetian kings to subdue their semi-independent vassals, and by the end of the thirteenth century institutions had already been developed for the subordination of local authorities, municipal as well as feudal, to the king's administration. The process had been gradual and uneven in its pace, and the system of administration had been very seriously weakened in the course of the recurrent wars with England. But after the end of the Hundred Years War, France very rapidly emerged as a more or less consolidated territorial monarchy. Although local privileges continued, and in some respects were even strengthened, the exercise of political authority was almost everywhere subject to the king's officials and his ' sovereign ' courts, either by direct intervention or appeal. Around the beginning of the sixteenth century, Louis XII and Francis I had already achieved sufficient control over the military and economic resources of the country to engage the Spanish monarchy in a contest for hegemony in Europe.

At least at the beginning of the century the politically articulate elements of French society either endorsed the strengthened monarchy or else were willing to adjust to it.[3] The Gallican Church had always depended on the king's protection and after the *Concordat* of 1516, which compromised its independence, appointments to the higher clergy had become even more dependent upon royal patronage. The high aristocrats had been able to compensate for declining independence with posts of influence and honor within the king's administration and to sustain their clienteles through access to the royal patronage. The lesser nobility, although still imbued with feudal attitudes and loyalties, increasingly depended on royal military service to sustain their social status. Within the educated bourgeoisie, many had found opportunity for wealth and social elevation in the king's judicial and administrative service. Within the towns, the higher bourgeoisie, although often dismayed by the fiscal burdens of the new regime, were too dependent upon royal favor and too much the beneficiaries of privileges granted by the crown to challenge the existing order on their own account.

But at the same time a basic political condition of the centralized regime was respect for rights of the community in general, and of the several provinces in particular. The consolidation of royal government could not have succeeded in the long run without the support, or at least neutrality, of the chartered towns, ecclesiastical corporations, and the lesser nobles, and the price of this support was the willingness and ability of the kings to guarantee existing privileges even more effectively than the feudatories they replaced. The privileged elements of any given region did not lose established rights when they

---

phase of French royalism is absorbed by the distinction between absolutism in the sense of royal supremacy and despotism in the sense of unlimited rights over persons and property.

[3] For a general discussion of the relation between social structure and politics in the sixteenth century, see Lucien Romier, *Le royaume de Catherine de Médicis*, 2 vols (Paris, 1925).

came into more direct relation to the crown. They exchanged the protection of the local overlord for the protection of the crown itself. This mutuality of obligation was often made explicit in contractual agreements between the king and the provincial estates when a province was annexed to the royal domain. With each accession of a new incumbent to the throne, the terms of these agreements were generally reconfirmed.

The ' Renaissance monarchy ' was thus expected to respect established law and not to alter it without consent. To this principle the government itself was committed in one form or another even though the risks were sometimes great. The fiscal burdens of the new regime, together with the social tensions that accompanied its growth, had created political resentments which could easily be crystallized if nationwide assemblies were called. For this reason the Estates General, which had been a forum for agitation against royal policy during the crises of the wars with England, were looked on with suspicion by the monarchs of the Renaissance and were not assembled from 1484 to 1560. Yet even so, the rule of consultation was observed through less volatile devices – through provincial or regional assemblies of the three estates, through regional or national assemblies of town delegations, through church assemblies, and also through nationwide assemblies of notables, essentially in the form of an expanded meeting of the king's Great Council, which provided a smaller, less formal, and therefore more readily manageable substitute for a full Estates assembly. But the idea of the Estates as the most solemn and beneficial form of consultation retained its vitality as a community tradition.[4]

Communication between the king and the community was not restricted to direct assemblies alone. It was also sustained, on a more continuing basis, by the mediation of the king's administration, which was not only an agency for enforcement of the royal will but an independent check upon its arbitrary exercise. In the Renaissance monarchy the complex and decentralized network of territorial officials was coordinated at the center by the great sovereign courts, which were technically offshoots of the royal council.[5] The oldest of these was the Parlement of Paris which was normally the court of final instance both for civil and criminal cases and for cases involving the powers and conduct of officials. In view of its multiple responsibilities, ecclesiastical as well as lay, the Parlement of Paris was divided into several chambers, some of which had become independent institutions except for certain forms. In the sixteenth century, however, it was still regarded as a single entity, and the

---

[4] For a survey of the elements of decentralization continuing in the Renaissance monarchy, see J. Russell Major, ' The Renaissance Monarchy: A Contribution to the Periodization of History ', *The Emory University Quarterly*, XIII, no. 2, June 1957, pp. 112–24, and also the first chapter of his *Representative Institutions in Renaissance France, 1421–1559* (Madison, 1960).

[5] Detailed surveys of French institutions in this period are Roger Doucet, *Les institutions politiques de la France au XVIe siècle* (Paris, 1948); and Gaston Zeller, *Les institutions politiques de la France au XVIe siècle* (Paris, 1948).

Great Chamber of the Parlement was the final instance of appeal and of political and administrative review. The Parlement of Paris, finally, was empowered, in principle at least, to hear appeals from the provincial Parlements which had been created, under varying names, beginning with the first quarter of the fifteenth century. Even though this procedure was now regarded as abusive and exceptional, the Parlement of Paris was above the others in prestige and its legal precedents were generally followed. In strictest theory the provincial Parlements were extensions of a single court.[6]

The officials of this apparatus were not regarded and did not behave as mere servants or dependents of the king. The most important officers were recruited from privileged strata which had an aristocratic sense of independence toward the crown. The *baillis* and *sénéschaux*, who were the more important local supervisors, were normally members of the fighting nobility, often chosen from the district they administered, and they carried out their duties with lieutenants and counsellors who were also often chosen from the area and who represented local interests. The sovereign courts, on the other hand, were increasingly staffed by legally educated members of the upper bourgeoisie, who might seem on that account to be more indebted to the king for the enhancement of their social status. But the Parlement of Paris was not strictly an appointive body since, in principle at least, the court was not required to receive a member unless it had examined and approved his qualifications.

According to what was regarded as the right procedure, the Parlement was virtually cooptative in that the king was expected to make any new appointment from a list of candidates selected by the existing membership. By this and other legal devices, high judicial offices tended to be passed on from generation to generation within a single family, so that we may already think of this elite as a highly privileged and quasi-hereditary *noblesse de robe*. This new *noblesse*, moreover, almost insensibly acquired further status from its association with the old. The Parlement was still regarded as a component of the royal council. It was also still the Court of Peers and might sometimes be attended by the peers of France when it sat in that capacity. Many of its counsellors were still recruited from the nobility and higher clergy.

This sense of independence was also promoted by the deeply rooted principle that crown officers were irremovable except for cause. In the Renaissance, as in the Middle Ages, office was a quasi-feudal dignity, the loss of which was

---

[6] For this reason the usage of this term varies greatly in the sources. ' Parlement ' may refer either to the Parlement of Paris alone, or to the Parlements collectively, or to all the sovereign courts (sometimes including the Great Council). Used historically it may refer to the entire council of the king in the early Middle Ages, with which the Three Estates is sometimes identified. I have not adopted any special nomenclature. In most cases I will be using the term to refer to the Parlement of Paris especially, without excluding broader reference to the regional Parlements. In most cases nuances of reference are not theoretically significant for present purposes. Important distinctions are indicated directly or by the context.

a violation of the holder's status. So long, therefore, as the office continued to exist in law, the appointee was irremovable except by a showing of misconduct to the courts. By the middle of the sixteenth century, the sale of judicial offices, formerly an occasional practice, had begun to be fairly common, and from Montesquieu on this has been interpreted as a prime source of judicial independence. But its importance ought not to be exaggerated. The sale of offices (which was bitterly protested by the Parlement as a violation of its honor) may well have strengthened pre-existing tendencies for office to become proprietary. Venality was not required to establish the irremovability of a particular incumbent, since this principle was already admitted universally.

The king's administration, furthermore, was not only independent in its status and its attitude, but had always held an exalted conception of its constitutional prerogatives. By the fifteenth century it was well established that the Parlement of Paris had the right to remonstrate, or protest, against any enactment of the king found incompatible with common law or local custom, unless the alteration could be justified by strong considerations of public utility or equity. This was understood as something much more solemn than mere apprisal of the king of consequences that he might have overlooked. The Parlement of Paris, together with the other sovereign courts, claimed the right to withhold registration of an act, and thus to prevent its promulgation as a binding law, until its remonstrations had been satisfied.[7] Reiterated commands to register, backed up by a variety of threats, might ultimately secure compliance. But registration by letter of command or by *lit de justice* was regarded as contrary to good practice and abusive, and enactments imposed by a command were sometimes recorded with the phrase *de mandato expresso*, by which the court declared that registration was unwilling and not completely binding. As we shall later see, the ultimate locus of authority in conflicts between king and Parlement was not yet clearly defined. In the sixteenth century cooperation of the two was presupposed, and exceptions to this norm ignored.[8]

The new monarchy of the later Middle Ages and the Renaissance thus presents a double aspect. One side of it was the gradual formation of a centralized administration which registered the triumph of the royal government over its older, feudal opposition. But the other side was the institutionalization, within that same administration, of the medieval principle that the king must

[7] ' And the kings have found it neither bad nor strange that the counsellors of the Parlement who judge and ought to judge according to their conscience, informed of the truth through law and reason, may have responded, in the verification of letters with which they were charged, that they were unable to proceed, and used these words: *Non possumus, non debemus* (we cannot, and we ought not).' Declaration of the Parlement of Paris, 5 December 1556, quoted by Edouard Maugis, *Histoire du Parlement de Paris de l'avènement des rois Valois à la mort d'Henri IV*, 3 vols (Paris, 1913–16), I, p. ix.

[8] For an account of the development of the right of remonstration and registration, as well as the practice of this period, see *ibid.* I, pp. 517–601.

govern with consent. This second side, no doubt, was not always accepted by the kings themselves. In periods of conflict with their Parlements they, or their chancellors, often argued that the functions of the courts were purely ministerial, and strong princes like Francis I and Henry II could sometimes act in defiance of restraints.[9] But the significant point for present purposes is that the element of limitation upon royal power continued to be recognized by most of the jurists of the time.

The opinions of these commentators reflect the ambiguity of the system they expound, and maintain a delicate balance between monarchist and constitutionalist ideas. If the former element sometimes seems overwhelming to the modern reader, it is because the lawyers are so heavily dependent on the terminology of Roman law. The status of Roman law in medieval France is a highly complicated question which need not be considered here. We need only observe that Roman legal concepts, as elaborated by the medieval commentators, had long been accepted by French jurists as the ordinary form of learned discourse. In this process the basic equation of the position of the king of France with that of the Roman *princeps* became the tacit starting point for all reflections. Toward the end of the thirteenth century, the legists had relied on this idea to articulate the independent status of the king with respect to the Pope and German Emperor. According to their celebrated formula, the king of France within his kingdom was its emperor (*Rex Franciae in suo regno est imperator sui regni*). At least in this sense, therefore, he was ' absolute '.

Furthermore, in the fourteenth and fifteenth centuries, the formulae of Roman law were increasingly used to shape and to rationalize the procedures of the central administration. The administration of the state was the administration of the prince, and the will of the prince was viewed as the source and impetus of the entire apparatus. Hence in this respect as well, his status seemed best described as ' absolute '.

For such reasons, the idea of ' absolute ' authority was universally accepted in French law, and the language of the commentators sometimes seems shockingly immoderate. One influential example is a work by Barthélemy de Chasseneuz, who was one of the most authoritative jurists of the early sixteenth century. In his *Catalogus gloriae mundi* (1529), 208 attributes of majesty are culled from the *Corpus Juris* and its medieval commentators, from the writings of the canon lawyers, and from medieval traditions of the sacred kingship; and these are listed and fulsomely embroidered in order to glorify the crown. Another example is the *Regalium Franciae libri duo* of Charles de

[9] The king could attempt to force registration by threats to suppress or remove the court as well as by threats against its members personally, and he could seek to avert judicial sabotage subsequent to registration by removing key cases to the royal council. The tactics of Francis I are described by Roger Doucet, *Étude sur le gouvernement de Francois Ier dans ses rapports avec le Parlement de Paris* (Paris, 1921) ch. III (on the reception of the *Concordat* of 1516).

Grassaille, who often follows Chasseneuz, and the flavor of this kind of rhetoric may be readily conveyed by reproducing selected chapter headings from this work:

The king of the French is a great lord and more glorious than any other king.

The king of France compared to all other kings and princes of this age is like the morning star amidst the northern cloud, and holds the crown of liberty and glory before all the other kings of this world.

The king of France is the vicar of Christ in his kingdom.

The king of France is called the king of kings.

The king of France is called a second sun on earth.

When the Pope and the king of France agree, they can do everything.

The kingdom of the French is held of God alone.

Although certain other kings are anointed, only the most Christian king is anointed by oil miraculously conveyed.

The king of France is called the delegated minister and vicar of God.

The king of France performs miracles in life and heals scrofula.

The king of France is like a corporeal god.[10]

Yet language of this sort is not to be construed in isolation. The imagery of absolutism was often used to glorify the cohesion and independence of the whole commonwealth considered as a *corpus mysticum*. If the ultimate power of the commonwealth was always located in the ruler as its head, this did not necessarily imply that he might invoke his absolute authority without the consent of other members. Even ' absolute ' authority was subjected to distinctions, as it were, and to the specification of cases where it could not be rightfully asserted. It was in this fashion that medieval notions of consent were grafted onto Roman maxims, sometimes where we least expect to find them. One of the most important constitutionalists of the early sixteenth century was Chasseneuz himself.

The constitutionalist doctrines of the jurists are most often expressed in comments on the status of the sovereign courts. The key to this literature is the assumption that the Parlement of Paris was a French version of the early Roman Senate. In Guymier's gloss of 1481 on the Pragmatic Sanction of Bourges, the Parlement is already said to have been formed on the model of the Roman Senate as Romulus was supposed to have created it.[11] The French Senate, like its Roman counterpart, contained a normal complement of just

---

[10] Charles de Grassaille, *Regalium Franciae libri duo* (1538) (Paris, 1545) index. (The index is simply a list of paragraph captions that appear in the margins of the text.) For the origins and development of these lists of privileges, which go back to the later fifteenth century, see Jacques Poujol, ' Jean Ferrault on the King's Privileges: A Study of the Medieval Sources of Renaissance Political Theory in France ', *Studies in the Renaissance*, 5 (1958) pp. 15–26. The earlier lists were based on the various privileges acknowledged by the papacy as accorded to the kings of France. By the time of Grassaille, there was a definite tendency to treat these powers as inherent.

[11] Cosme Guymier, *Pragmatica Sanctio una cum reportorio* (1486) (Paris, 1504) fos cciv–ccv.

one hundred members when all of its components were assembled, and in subsequent literature its counsellors are referred to as ' senatores ' or ' patres ' because of their venerable authority. By 1500 this comparison had become standard in the legal commentators, and the high status of the Roman Senate was regularly invoked to explain the great dignity and splendor of the Parlement.

For this purpose the most suggestive passage in the *Corpus Juris* was *Code* 9, 8, 5 (*ad legem Juliam majestatis*), which defined the crime of treason. The bearers of majesty protected by the rule include not only the person of the Emperor but also ' the illustrious men who are in our councils and consistory, and especially the Senators (for they are part of our body) '. Hence for French lawyers the Parlement, or Senate of France, was likewise *pars corporis principis* or *regis*, a part of the prince's body politic. Although created by the king, and after him in precedence, the Parlement was associated in his dignity and status, and it is sometimes referred to as his peer or equal. ' It is also to be pointed out ', says Grassaille, ' that the

king must do them honors ... and that they ought to sit not at the feet of the prince but at his side. .... For the Chancellor and the Senators are the prince's soul and make it possible for the kings to reign (*et reges faciunt regnare*).[12]

It is this conception that suggests the true meaning of the lists of regalian dignities composed by Chasseneuz and others. The absolute powers of the king were possessed and shared in various degrees by all the high components of the *corpus mysticum*.

The proof and expression of the ' Senate's ' majesty were its high judicial prerogatives, which were ' royal ' or ' sovereign ' in character. The Parlement, acting as a court, was like the Roman Senate or, at times, the Pretorian Prefect of the Emperor, in that its decrees were considered to be final.[13] In principle at least (if not in practice uniformly) there was no recourse from its verdict to the king. The only proper basis for appeal was a supplication for rehearing presented to the Parlement itself.[14] According to the jurists, the decrees of the Parlements were called *arresta*, in order to indicate their ultimacy.[15] Moreover, in contrast with the decrees of lower magistrates, whose authority was less than ' sovereign ', the *arresta* of the Parlements were pronounced in their own name, not the king's.[16]

The Parlements, furthermore, were possessed of the sovereign prerogative to act against, or without, established law in order to provide equitable relief, especially in civil litigation. They could remove cases from inferior jurisdic-

---

12 Grassaille, *Regalium Franciae*, p. 112.

13 *Ibid.* pp. 116–17. Grassaille's extended discussion of the Parlement's high powers is a *summa* of earlier opinion on this point. All or most of his attributions are to be found in each of the following: Montaigne, Budé, Benoist, and Chasseneuz. The discussions of the Parlements by these other writers will be cited below for other points.   14 *Ibid.* p. 117.

15 *Ibid.*   16 *Ibid.*

tions at their own discretion.[17] They were not restricted to the specific questions raised by the complaints and petitions laid before them.[18] In rendering judgments they were not bound to all ' the solemnities and subtleties of law ', but might judge according to their conscience.[19] In criminal cases they could commute or lower sentences, and in civil matters they could undo the effects of contracts on equitable grounds.[20] Unlike the Roman Senate, the Parlements could not declare oblivion for crimes, or increase the statutory punishments. Both of these prerogatives were reserved entirely to kings.[21] But the Parlements were accorded considerable power to dispense with statutory law and, along with this, a certain authority to change its rules. The Senate of France, it was generally agreed, had some share of the power to make law, as did the Roman Senate and the Pretorian Prefect, although unlike these latter, the Parlements could legislate only with the specific authorization of the king.[22]

Thus, with one or two exceptions,[23] the Parlement was conceived by the jurists as a great center of sovereign authority alongside of, and all but equal to, the king. This conception is all the more significant because it was always assumed that its counsellors were not removable except for cause.[24]

Up to this point, these glorifications of the Parlement are mostly an assimilation of its functions to those of the Senate of imperial Rome. The critical difference, however, is the further insistence by the French that the Parlement, created by the king, was empowered to disallow his acts, to which power there was no parallel in Roman law. The closest approximation was *Code* I, 14, 8 (*l. humanum*) in which Theodosius and Valentinian informed the Senate that there was no better way to insure the justice of laws and rescripts than to submit them to the Senate for examination and to withhold enactment unless a majority of that body gave approval. The declaration concludes with the assurance that ' in the future no law is to be promulgated in any other way by our clemency '.

The gloss compiled in the middle of the thirteenth century took this last to mean that the Emperors had promised to make no further changes in the body of the law. But the later commentators took a more sophisticated view. According to Bartolus, the procedure of *l. humanum* was ' not of necessity, but will, so that its omission does not vitiate a law ',[25] and he is confirmed in this by all the later writers.

---

[17] *Ibid*. p. 122.   [18] *Ibid*. p. 120.   [19] *Ibid*. pp. 118, 124.

[20] *Ibid*. pp. 120, 122.   [21] *Ibid*. pp. 122, 127.   [22] *Ibid*. p. 117.

[23] A notable exception is Nicholas Bohier, *Tractatus de ordine et praecedentia graduum utriusque fori* in *Tractatus universi juris* (Venice, 1584-6) XVI, fos 265r-72v. Bohier emphatically states the priority of King-in-Great Council on the grounds that cases could be evoked there from any other court including the Parlements. Bohier, a member of the Parlement of Toulouse, was perhaps jealous of the Parlement of Paris and looked more to the Great Council (of which he was also a member) as the center of the state. In any event his view is exceptional for this period.   [24] Grassaille, *Regalium Franciae*, p. 124.

[25] *Commentarii*, II vols (Venice, 1590) V, f. 28v. Also his comment on *Digest* I, I, 9 (*l. omnes populi*): ' And if high judges and lords should do this [i.e. make statutes], it is the part

The French, on the other hand, were persuaded that there was something inherently improper about a royal order that had not been ratified. The importance of consultation and consent was deeply rooted in medieval thought, and appears in the civilian commentators as well as in the customary lawyers. But the French were particularly emphatic on this point, and one of the strongest expressions in the first decade of the sixteenth century was by the humanist Guillaume Budé, who came close to making examination and approval a legal requirement. In his *Annotationes* to the *Digest*, which was the first sustained attempt at a philological study of the texts, Budé included a long digression comparing the French Parlement with the Senate of Rome in the republican as well as the imperial period. In Budé's judgment the republican Senate had possessed the power of ratifying and confirming legislation by the people, and this he believed was the proper analogue to the function of the Parlement of France:

Furthermore, just as when the people had approved of something (whence it was called a plebiscite [i.e. from *sciscente*, in *plebe sciscente*], the Senate was properly required as its sponsor (*Senatorem auctorem fieri oportebat*), which procedure we now refer to by the Greek derivative, homologate – so also with the ordinances of princes in order to be taken as inviolable sanctions (*ut vim sanctionum habeant*) . . . By its [the Parlement's] authority the acts of princes are confirmed or disconfirmed in order to forestall objections to them. This is the one court from which absolute princes take the law in a civil frame of mind, and which they would like to have as sponsor in the ratifying and promulgation of decrees. They would not wish to exempt their ordinances and edicts from the scrutiny of this council, but would rather see their enactments sanctified for all eternity by its decrees.[26]

Despite the boldness of this rhetoric, Budé is relatively cautious. He does not specify the legal consequence of ratification, or insist that it was indispensable. Yet even so his position was suggestive. The use of the early republican Senate as the analogue, rather than the much weaker imperial counterpart, implied that approval by the Parlement was intrinsic to the governmental process. The approval of the Senate was invariably sought, and acts which it had not endorsed were of doubtful standing in the courts.

Somewhat similar ideas are also encountered in the commentaries of Nicholas Bohier. In one respect, Bohier's position is an exception to the trend we are examining. On his account the highest center of adjudication and consent in France was not the Parlement, or Senate, but the Great Council, or the king's ' consistory ', which was a less defined as well as less independent body in view of its closer relation to the person of the king. Nevertheless, the

of humanity that they do it with advice as is indicated by . . . [*Code*, 1, 14, 4 (*l. digna vox*)]. But if they wish they can do this on their own motion (*proprio motu*) and promulgate it to their subjects.' *Commentarii*, 1, f. 9r. Baldus de Ubaldis, commentary on *Code* 1, 19, 6, *Praelectiones in Codicem* (Lyon, 1556), 1, f. 71r. gives a similar opinion.

[26] Guillaume Budé, *Annotationes in quatuor et viginti Pandectarum libros* (1507) (Paris, 1535) pp. 127–8.

Great Council, as Bohier understood it, was a large and public body with formal procedures and a weighty personnel, and he vigorously insisted that the king of France 'does nothing without his Great Council'. He even observes that the forms of consent, which were optional in Roman law, are observed unfailingly in France, which is almost to suggest that these procedures have become required through long-established usage:

Hence the form mentioned by the Emperor in *lex humanum* [*Code* 1, 14, 8] is observed in the kingdom of France. For whenever my supreme and most Christian lord wishes to make a statute, he convenes many prelates, governors, as well as counsellors of the Parlements of his kingdom to meet with himself and his Great Council . . . In this assembly led by the most illustrious and eminent Chancellor of France, he makes, promulgates, and establishes the propositions, laws, and constitutions which we call royal ordinances, just as he did in this year, 1510, for the orders passed by him and published at Lyon. And we see that this procedure has been kept by all the kings of France, his predecessors, and this is also attested by the proemium to the Pragmatic Sanction.[27]

But the idea of consultation as a norm was to be given even greater force and depth with the introduction of a specific theory of historical origins. One of the most influential sources for the jurists, along with the gloss on the Pragmatic Sanction, was the account of the origins of the Parlement in Gaguin's history of France, which appeared in 1491. According to Gaguin, the Parlement of Paris was the lineal descendant of an older council that had been instituted by Charles Martel. This original Parlement, or council, was supposed to have assembled the entire people, although at a rather early date, according to Gaguin, attendance was confined to persons skilled in law and well informed of custom, who were drawn from all the major regions of the kingdom. In these early days the Parlement met annually, and most often at a different place each year depending on the movements of the king. But in later times it was settled at Paris as a permanent court so that it could discharge its business more effectively. This business was primarily judicial in Gaguin's description. But he makes it very clear that then, as in the past, the Parlement was the natural place for reviewing laws and administrative measures, and that its consent was indispensable. 'The authority of this Parlement', he says, 'was always so great among the French that even the decisions of the king himself on public affairs, and on the law and finances of the kingdom, do not proceed without the decree of this Senate.'[28]

In the 1520s this theory of origins was taken over by many of the jurists. Gaguin's account is repeated verbatim by Guillaume Benoist,[29] and through

---

[27] Nicholas Bohier, *Additiones* to Jean Montaigne, *Tractatus de parlamentis et collatione parlamentorum* in *Tractatus universi juris* (Venice, 1584–6) xvi (fos 272r–7v) f. 274r.

[28] Robert Gaguin, *Compendium super Francorum gestis* (1491) (s. l. 1511) fos xlvii–xlviii.

[29] Guillaume Benoist (Benedictus), *Repetitio in cap. Raynutius, extra de testamentis et uxorem nomine Adelasiam* (1522) (Lyon, 1583) I, Dec. II, f. 84v.

Benoist it influenced Chasseneuz as well.[30] The idea of a specific date of origin suggests the notion of a deliberate promise to maintain the custom of consent, and reinforces the holding of both lawyers that consent is virtually necessary.

In the thinking of this period, moreover, the idea of limitations on the king was also applied to his judicial and executive prerogatives. In French procedure, and in monarchical procedure generally, the technical form of a remedy for civil injuries was a letter granted by the ruler in response to the request of a petitioner. Requests by a petitioner might also take the form of a claim to special privilege or to a gift of public funds. The king – in what might be called his executive capacity – was entitled to exempt from law and to bestow resources for good cause. In almost every case the king would issue such decrees or letters in full anticipation that they would then be subject to judicial scrutiny. The interesting question, therefore, was whether, if the king desired, he could preclude examination by the courts or override their judgment.

In the older civil law tradition, his ultimate power to do so was unquestioned. According to certain passages of *Code* I, titles 19, 22, 23, the courts were empowered, and enjoined, to refuse enforcement of any rescript of the Emperor that was in conflict with general ordinances. Hence rescripts elicited by fraud, in contravention of the common law or public interest, harmful to the public treasury, or doing serious injury to other parties could ordinarily be disallowed. But according to the medieval jurists the right to disallow did not obtain if the Emperor had clearly indicated that he wished to circumvent the courts. The right of the courts, in other words, did not affect the *plenitudo potestatis* of the prince, or his absolute and extraordinary power to make and to control the law, as distinguished from his *potestas ordinaria* or *moderata*. Where, in a rescript presented to the court, *plenitudo potestatis* was deliberately invoked, the right to disallow was set aside, and the rescript had to be enforced.

Various formulae for invoking *plenitudo potestatis* were developed by the medievals from hints and suggestions in the Roman texts.[31] By a *clausula ex proprio motu* the prince could certify that he was acting on his own motion and not merely as a favor to petitioner. There was no reason, therefore, to examine his command for fraud. By a *clausula ex certa scientia* he could assure the court that he had come to his decision, whether at the request of a

---

30 There is no reference to this account in the brief general description of the Parlements in the *Consuetudines Ducatus Burgundiae*, which was published before the appearance of Benoist's work. Chasseneuz follows Benoist, however, in the *Catalogus gloriae mundi* (1529) (Geneva, 1649) pp. 280–1.

31 These formulae, which seem to have been initially developed by the canonists, have innumerable nuances of meaning, and may often be used interchangeably. The latter is especially true of *proprius motus* and *certa scientia*. The rendition following is frequent in the civilians and is sufficient for present purposes. The technical meaning of the term will not usually be important.

petitioner or not, only after deliberate reflection, which normally implied advice. There could thus be no occasion to examine his narrative of fact or law. By a *clausula non-obstante*, finally, the prince could indicate that he wished his command to be obeyed, previous legislation notwithstanding.[32] In the most formidable and complex of *non-obstante* clauses, the law, or laws, to be excepted were particularly mentioned.[33]

But among French jurists of the early sixteenth century, there was a cautious but definite tendency to hold that *plenitudo potestatis* could not be legitimately invoked in derogation of a rule of law that the people had accepted and the ruler had confirmed. Thus at one point in his *Consuetudines Ducatus Burgundiae*, Chasseneuz considers the legal status of Burgundian customs. The customary law of this province, like that of many others, had been collected by order of the king, approved and edited by the provincial estates, and then confirmed by royal act. Noting this status, Chasseneuz inquires whether custom thus confirmed can be set aside by royal letters:

In the first place, the customs of our Duchy of Burgundy have been approved by our most Christian king, and he has sworn to honor them as laws. Furthermore, they were enacted in a convocation of the Three Estates of our province [i.e. Burgundy] and have thus acquired the force of a pragmatic sanction. By virtue of this fact they cannot be derogated from by any clause that can be affixed. And by virtue of this fact that they have been confirmed by the prince, they cannot be suspended or suffer derogation by means of a *non-obstante* clause. The *non-obstante* clause cannot suspend a custom or disposition confirmed by the prince.[34]

A moment later Chasseneuz expresses hesitation:

And because our customs have been sworn to by the prince, who has sworn at his entry and accession (*iuravit in introitu et adventu*) to keep the statutes, privileges, and customs of our land [Burgundy], he cannot therefore be presumed to suspend them by a *non-obstante* clause. . . So the prince cannot do this, unless he may do it

---

[32] Thus Bartolus on derogation from civil law in general, ' I ask, thirdly, whether the prince may issue a rescript contrary to civil law [i.e. as distinguished from higher law]. Here observe what the gloss has to say. Either the prince wishes to prescribe (*rescribere*) against common law in an act of legislation, and can do so . . . Or he wishes to grant someone a privilege, and can grant it, if the privilege harms another only slightly. If it injures another immoderately, he cannot grant it . . . If it injures no one, then he can grant it . . . If it is harmful to the public, he cannot grant it . . . But I ask, what if the prince prescribes against law, but says it shall be valid, the laws notwithstanding – is this required? The gloss says yes. Others say that it is not required, so long as he knows that he is prescribing against law . . . But that . . . [applies] to rescripts granting benefices and not to a privilege and so is not relevant here. We may generally hold that he must insert that clause . . . And I think it is not enough for him to say, " anything notwithstanding ", because that is a general utterance. Likewise, I think he is not required to say " notwithstanding such and such law ", actually naming it, because that is a particular or individual utterance. It is enough for him to say, " notwithstanding any law to the contrary ". That is a special utterance.' Commentary on *Code* I, 22, 6, *Commentarii*, VII, f. 34r.

[33] See Baldus de Ubaldis, *Praelectiones in Codicem*, I. f. 71v, for a rich but condensed account of the general theory of derogation.

[34] *Consuetudines Ducatus Burgundiae* (1517) (Geneva, 1615) col. 1534 (*tit. de retractatibus*).

by his *plenitudo potestatis*. As to whether he can or not, I find no clear opinion in the doctors [of Roman civil law]... In any event [the invocation of] *plenitudo potestatis* is never to be presumed... unless it is expressly mentioned... And Jason [da Mayno] says the prince should use this clause only rarely... and that the Roman people [in the republic] never used it. Nor is there any specific reference to this form in the Civil Law [*Corpus Juris*] as Baldus says.[35]

This second passage is far from a retraction of the first. Chasseneuz is insisting that if confirmed custom can be detracted from at all, the most specific of *non-obstante* clauses is needed, which is a kind most difficult to operate.[36] Even then the possibility is left in doubt. If Chasseneuz does not go all the way to flat denial, it is because he is no more prepared than any other jurist of this period to remove that ultimate residual sense in which the king of France is absolute.

But the best known statement of the king's subjection to the law is from Seyssel's *Monarchie de France*. This formulation is a few years earlier than Chasseneuz's; but I have postponed it to this point in order to clarify its legal implication.[37] Although Seyssel himself was a learned jurist, the *Monarchie de France* was not intended as a formal legal treatise. It was an attempt to present the custom and practice of the kingdom as they actually worked politically. As a result of this method and this interest, Seyssel is at once more flexible and less precise. But the underlying legal thought is much the same as in the jurists.

In the *Monarchie de France* three checks on royal power are distinguished. The third of these, along with religion and justice, is what Seyssel calls ' la police ':

The third check is police; which is to say the various ordinances that have been made by the kings themselves and afterwards confirmed and approved from time to time, and which tend to the preservation of the kingdom as a whole and of its parts. These have been so well kept for so long a time that the princes do not derogate from them. And when they would have wished to do so, their commands were not obeyed. This is especially true when it comes to their domain and royal patrimony which they cannot alienate except in circumstances of necessity and only if the alienation is examined and approved by the sovereign courts of the Parlements or by the Chamber of Accounts. These courts proceed so deliberately and raise so many issues and difficulties that few men would purchase such alienations, knowing that they would neither be valid nor guaranteed.[38]

This passage must be read with caution since Seyssel could well have been thinking of dilatory tactics by the court rather than an outright veto. Yet even

---

35 *Ibid.*

36 Chasseneuz also insists that if the clause is to be used it must be issued by the king personally, not by his chancellor. *Consuetudines*, col. 1535.

37 Chasseneuz, it may be noted, had once studied law under Seyssel at Turin.

38 Claude de Seyssel, *La monarchie de France* (1519) Jacques Poujol, ed. (Paris, 1961) p. 119.

so, its underlying point is clear. Where legislation had been ratified, either by the procedures mentioned in Bohier or Budé, or else by long approval and reiteration by the kings themselves, a kind of promise had been given by the king that restricted his *plenitudo potestatis*. Since Seyssel was learned in Roman law, the phrase ' when they would have wished to do so ' would seem to refer to derogatory clauses. The validity of these is not excluded absolutely, for the mood of the succeeding phrase, ' their commands were not obeyed ', is formally indicative. Yet the sense is cautiously imperative. Seyssel, like Chasseneuz, is tactfully saying that *plenitudo potestatis* is not and may not be invoked, even though its ultimate existence cannot be denied.

One consequence of this conception of the rule of law was the right of the courts to repudiate orders of the king in the ordinary course of doing justice. French commentators often boasted that the rule of law was more rigorously observed in France than in any other country, and this implied that all letters and edicts of the king, directly affecting the rights of individuals, were automatically subject to examination to test their conformity with law. This would apply not only to the various letters of justice issued by the chancellery, and acquired by petitioners to institute proceedings, but also to grants of privilege which adversely affected the rights of other parties and could therefore be contested in the courts. For this domain, the subjection of the king to law seemed so fundamental to the commentators that they often insisted upon it without the slightest hint of reservations.

Here again the most celebrated statement is Seyssel's:

[T]he second [check] is justice, which, without doubt, is better authorized in France than in any country that we know in all the world. This is especially owing to the Parlements, which have been instituted for this reason and this purpose: – to put a bridle on the absolute power that our kings would have wished to use. And so, from the beginning, persons were established of such eminence, and in such number, and with such power that the kings have always been subject to them so far as distributive justice is concerned. This goes so far that a man can obtain right and justice against them [i.e. the kings] just as he can against their subjects, at least in civil cases. And in cases between private parties, the kings' authority cannot prejudice another's right, but their letters and rescripts are subject to the judgment of the aforesaid Parlements in such a case, and they are examined not only for misrepresentation and fraud (as are those of other princes according to the Roman law) but are also judged for their legality and illegality [i.e. for their consistency with well-established law].[39]

[39] *Ibid.* pp. 117–18. The last phrase on judgment for ' legality and illegality ' is frequently mentioned in the sixteenth century as an important difference between French and Roman practice. According to Ugo Nicolini, *La proprietá, il principe, e l'espropriazione per publica utilitá* (Milan, 1940) pp. 183ff, this very narrow interpretation of the Roman rule goes back to the position of the very early French civilian, Placentinus, who read the passage ' contra jus elicita ' as applying only to rescripts *obtained* in an illegal manner as opposed to rescripts that in themselves were uncivil or against the law, p. 183. The Italian civilians regularly assume that both defects invalidate the case of the rescript's recipient. The difference is not

In Chasseneuz the same idea is given even greater force. The regular magistrates of France are described as the ephors and tribunes of the realm. Despite their appointment by the king, they are portrayed as people's protectors, who have been vested with the power to veto decrees against the law. But the remarks of Grassaille, who copies Chasseneuz in this, are perhaps the most fulsome of them all:

Thirdly, adherence to justice by the kings of France is shown by this. Although Pope, king, and Emperor have the power to judge in their own cause . . . the kings of France submit themselves, of their own accord, to the judgment of their *baillis* and *sénéschaux*. The kings invariably obey the judgments of these officers. And they [the kings] will and order that their letters be sent to them [the officers] for execution, just as Valerian writes of Theopompus, king of the Spartans, who created those magistrates known as ephors, similar to the tribunes of the people at Rome, for the purpose of restraining (*moderandam*) his royal will . . . Since the wills of kings are impulsive, and often vacillate and contradict themselves . . . the kings of France have ordained and declared through many constitutions and ordinances that letters emanating from them can be publicly and judicially impugned in declared judgment for any nullity, inequity, or fraud.[40]

The general tendencies may thus be summarized as follows: The king of France is absolute in principle. But by many promises, implicit or express, he has undertaken not to invoke his *plenitudo potestatis*. He may not, therefore, alter well-established law without the advice and consent of some proper version of the early Parlement; he may not detract from law in an illegal manner; and we have also seen that he may not evade judicial scrutiny by evoking cases for his own consideration.[41] If he should seek to violate these promises, his wish is not to be presumed deliberate.

In the period before and right after the middle of the sixteenth century, when royal dominance was at its height, expressions of such views were more timid and are less frequently encountered. Grassaille, in 1538, was sometimes less explicit than his predecessors, particularly on forms of legislation. Pierre Rebuffi, commenting on royal ordinances just before the middle of the century, alludes to the earlier ideas at one point or another, but does so guardedly and wistfully.[42] Yet even so there was no real breach of continuity.

very important. The French assume that when the terms of a rescript are illegal, this fact may also be taken as *prima facie* evidence that petitioner has obtained it by misrepresentation (*obreptio*). The Parlements often use the same idea to attack royal ordinances. If they are manifestly ' bad ', the king must have been misled by corrupt advisers or petitioners.

40 Grassaille, *Regalium Franciae*, pp. 204–5.

41 See above, p. 8. Although evocations and irregular appeals often occurred where cases were highly sensitive politically, the Parlement bitterly protested, and there were promises in many royal ordinances that the king would refrain from such practices in the future. The earlier jurists thus assume the finality of decisions in the Parlement as the normal rule. For the reasons we have indicated, Bohier is an exception.

42 Pierre Rebuffi, *Commentarii in constitutiones seu ordinationes regias* (1549) 3 vols (Lyon, 1554) II, p. 455: ' You see here that this good king used to make and publish laws by

The constitutionalist interpretation of the powers of the king was not so much denied as tactfully passed over.

But in the decade after 1560, when feeble incumbents to the throne confronted growing opposition, the earlier ideas were not only revived but more vigorously stated.[43] The greater boldness of this later period is methodological as well as substantive. The new school of French antiquarians, building on Seyssel's approach, no longer went directly to the *Corpus Juris*, or to the glosses of its medieval commentators, for the understanding of French public law, and this was a significant departure from the procedures of the older jurists. Commentators like Bohier or Chasseneuz may be considered ' French civilians ', when writing on domestic law, because they depend on Roman authority as much as possible to expound their legal maxims. But antiquarian writers, like Pasquier or Du Haillan, took custom, and the history of custom, as the starting point, and they were thus committed by their very method to finding divergencies from Roman principles.[44] The same applies, it may be noted, to the new school of comparative politics and law, of which the leading representatives were Bodin and Louis le Roy. For them too, the equivalence of French and Roman law was something to be discovered rather than assumed.

In its substance, the earlier doctrine was basically unchanged, except that among many of the antiquarians the historic promises of the kings of France were given even greater force and emphasis. It is thus in Etienne Pasquier that Seyssel's idea of verification was to receive its most precise and classic formulation:

It is a truly a great thing, and becoming to a prince's majesty,[45] that our kings (to

consent of the Three Estates and it would be good if this were done today. For the Three Estates are in place of the people, and if the people cannot meet all together, the Senate should be consulted in place of them, as the text says [*Digest* 1, 2, 9]. The three estates are the clergy, the nobles, and the commoners, and in the province of Narbonne they have been assembled every year up to now. But whether the Estates would advance the people's welfare today they alone know who will have to explain to God on high some day, if they do not assemble them. We know full well, however, that if this were ordered with your council, it would redound to the happiness of our state and to our glory.' See also 1, pp. 21–2, where a similar thought is expressed with citation to Benoist.

43 I shall be dealing here only with the more scholarly literature, on which see also Church, *Constitutional Thought*, ch. 3 *passim*. The influence of Seyssel in general, including the polemical literature, is also documented in the excellent study of the movement of political ideas in this later period by Vittorio de Caprariis, *Propaganda e pensiero politico in Francia durante le guerre di religione*, I, *1559–1572* (Naples, 1959).

44 For an account of this school and its contributions to historiography, see Donald R. Kelley, *Foundations of Modern Historical Scholarship : Language, Law, and History in the French Renaissance* (New York and London, 1970) chs VIII–X. Pasquier (who is probably the most eminent representative) and Du Haillan I have singled out for treatment here because it is in them that the Seysselian trend endemic in this school was most clearly expressed.

45 This phrase is inspired by *Code* 1, 14, 4 (*l. digna vox*) but without citations. The declaration by Theodosius and Valentian that it is ' the voice of decency in him who rules to profess that he is bound by law ' is endlessly quoted in this period, although for almost every constitutional position.

whom God gave absolute and plenary power) have willed to subject their wills to the civility of law, and so to have their edicts pass through the alembic of this public order [i.e. the Parlements]. And something even more remarkable is that as soon as some ordinance has been published and verified by the Parlement, the French people immediately adhere to it ungrudgingly, as if this company was the link and tie between the obedience of the people and the commands of the prince.[46]

Pasquier, moreover, is even more explicit than Seyssel in extending this procedure to acts of legislation. He now explicitly asserts that the royal promise goes not only to particular decrees but also to his general determinations, or *volontez générales*:

For just as nothing of importance to the kingdom was undertaken under Charlemagne or his successors without assembling the prelates and barons to examine the affair, so when the Parlement was stabilized, it was considered right (*fut trouvé bon*) that the general determinations of our kings should not obtain the force of edicts unless they were verified and homologated in that place. Originally this procedure was followed without hypocrisy or dissimulation.[47]

Pasquier, like Seyssel and Chasseneuz, is not quite willing to hold that use of *puissance absolue* is excluded altogether. He notes, unhappily, that *lettres de jussion* occur and that there is little to be done against them, and his attitude is much the same on the use of evocations.[48] Yet even so, he clearly indicates that both practices are recent and abusive. In the case of letters imposed upon the court, he endorses the practice of registering them with the notation ' by express command ', which shows that the court has disapproved.[49] What he most desires is that both parties should show more consideration. He obviously feels that conflicts between king and court, made public by *lettres de jussion* and by the refusal of the court to give its sponsorship, must undermine respect for law and threaten the entire system.

But Du Haillan, who usually follows Pasquier closely, significantly omits

---

[46] Etienne Pasquier, *Les recherches de la France* (the second book in which political institutions are treated and to which all citations here are made was published in 1565) (Paris, 1607) p. 83.

[47] *Ibid.* p. 81.

[48] The *lettre de jussion* was an express order to the court enjoining it to register and execute an order to which it had previously objected, and was thus similar to the *lit de justice*, when used for this purpose. The *lettre de jussion* was a particularly virulent form of *plenitudo potestatis* since it overruled deliberate findings of defect by the Parlement. The clause is unknown in Roman law, although it was sometimes related to *Novellae*, Const. XVII (*Authenticae*, *Collat.* III, tit. 4) which does speak of second commands. According to Isambert, *Recueil général des ancienne lois françaises*, 29 vols (Paris, 1821–33) vi, pp. 703ff, it was first used in France in 1392. *Lettres de jussion* played a basic role in the struggle of Francis I to secure ratification of the *Concordat* of 1516.

Pasquier believed that among the first who attempted ' to force the consciences ' of the court was that ' ancient scourge of France ', Jean Sans Peur, Duke of Burgundy, in the early fifteenth century (*Recherches*, p. 81). On evocations, see *ibid.* p. 106. He is thinking here mainly of the expense of removals to the litigants.

[49] *Ibid.* pp. 82–3. The formula for receiving, and protesting, a forced registration is also mentioned in Rebuffi, *Commentarii*, II, 17.

his observation on forced registration. Reproducing a very strong opinion by Seyssel, he manages to suggest that *lettres de jussion* need not be accepted by the court, that remonstrations may continue nonetheless, and that the king must ultimately yield to reason in view of his promise of ' civilité '. The opening for *puissance absolue* is not completely closed, but is so narrowed that it almost vanishes:

All these things exist to restrain the disordered will of an impulsive prince so firmly that the inevitable result in the long run is that there is the time and means to make him change his mind before his unreasonable command is executed, or on that account to block him. If an improper decree is sometimes executed, suitable compensation is given afterwards (where reparation is possible), or at the very least the evil ministers (without whom princes would scarcely ever do evil things) are punished, so that it may be a lesson to those who come after them. This form of procedure has been so long observed in this kingdom that a prince, no matter how depraved, would be ashamed to violate it, and his various subjects and advisers would be afraid to advise him to do so or to lend him approval if he did. From this it follows that the sovereign and monarchical power of the kings is regulated and moderated by honest and reasonable means which these kings have introduced and have almost always observed.[50]

The trend of Du Haillan's opinion is thus in the direction of an outright veto. At the beginning of the seventeenth century, de la Roche-Flavin, in his massive summary of the Parlementaire tradition, flatly holds that acts which the Parlements have not approved are void.[51]

One further difference with the newer school is a broadened conception of community consent. In both Pasquier and Du Haillan the Estates are given

---

[50] Bernard de Girard (Du Haillan), *De l'estat et succez des affaires de France* (1570) (Paris, 1571) pp. 80–1. Cf. Seyssel, *Prohème en la translation de l'Histoire d'Appien*, in Poujol, ed., *La monarchie de France*, pp. 81–2. The same idea, in slightly weaker form, is expressed by Pasquier in an earlier work:

' And even assuming that they [royal letters granting gifts] are of his [the king's] own motion (*de son mouvement*), they would not obtain finality without great difficulty, for this court [the Parlement] has always reserved the liberty of making remonstrations in order to make him understand that his motions must (*doivent*) accord with reason. Otherwise, under the cover of a stolen clause, numerous favorites would turn their passion into law.' *Pourparler du prince* (Paris, 1560) p. 99. The same idea, but slightly weaker still, appears in Rebuffi, *Commentarii*, II, 17. The idea that French Parlements are particularly vigorous in protests and that kings usually acquiesce is stated somewhat more strongly in Bodin's earlier work on the state. See below, pp. 37–8.

[51] Bernard de la Roche-Flavin, *Treze livres des Parlemens de France* (Bordeaux, 1617) 13, ch. 17, n. 3, p. 702: ' Thus the first and principal authority of said Parlements is to verify the ordinances and edicts of the king; and such is the law of the kingdom that no edicts and no ordinances have any effect, and they are not obeyed – or rather they are not considered edicts or ordinances – unless they are verified by the sovereign courts, and by their free deliberation.'

On the other hand, it should be noted that Pasquier may have moved the other way and abandoned his earlier position in one of the very last pieces that he wrote. *De l'authorité royale* (1615) in Estienne Pasquier, *Ecrits politiques*, Dorothy Thickett ed. (Geneva, 1966) pp. 287–309. His views on the Parlement were now much the same as those of Bodin in the *République*, to which Pasquier frequently refers.

recognition as a version of the public council. Pasquier, skeptical as usual, comments sourly on the expectations of reform with which an Estates assembly was usually associated. The only thing permanent that seemed to come from them was an increase in the burden of taxation. Yet he does regard them as an alternative form of consultation, and undertakes exploration of their origins.[52]

With Du Haillan, on the other hand, the Estates are accorded a more fundamental constitutional position. He supposes that at the time of Philip the Fair, when the Parlement was settled at Paris, two additional bodies were created. Since the Parlement was now primarily designed for hearing private litigations,[53] the Great Council was created for continuing political advice.[54] At the same time a new assembly was called for hearing public grievances. On Du Haillan's account this third assemblage was thus the direct continuation of the original ambulatory council:

And to come back to the meaning of the term, Parlement: Inasmuch as public complaints and grievances were treated in those first Parlements, and since the Parlement of Paris, as it was instituted by Philip the Fair, had cognizance only of civil and criminal cases in last resort and without appeal, the aforesaid public grievances, complaints, and remonstrations were assigned to an assembly that was established at that time and called the Three Estates, while the name Parlement remained with the assembly of sovereign courts. . . .

After the convocation of the Estates had been instituted, our kings introduced the custom of holding them frequently, and undertook no great enterprise without consulting them, in imitation of our first kings who assembled the Parlement for resolving affairs of consequence. To hold an Estates is the same thing as formerly to hold a Parlement. It is nothing other than for the king to communicate with his subjects on affairs of very great moment, to take their counsel and advice, and to hear their complaints and grievances in order to provide for these as reason indicates.[55]

Some years later this idea is carried one step further. In his *Histoire générale des roys de France*, Du Haillan identifies the three Estates with the original version of the Parlement as established by the early Carolingians.[56] This alteration of chronology tended to enhance the prestige of the Estates and Du Haillan's account of 1576 could have been influenced by Hotman's *Franco-*

[52] Pasquier, *Recherches*, pp. 108ff.
[53] But not to the exclusion of power of verifying legislation. See, for example, Du Haillan, *De l'estat* . . . , pp. 87–8. No commentator of this period seriously discusses the right of the court to review ordinances approved by the Estates. This, however, was beginning to become an issue. See Church, *Constitutional Thought*, p. 139.
[54] Du Haillan, *De l'estat* . . . , p. 90.
[55] *Ibid.* pp. 88–9.
[56] Bernard de Girard (Du Haillan), *Histoire générale des roys de France* (1576) 2 vols (Paris, 1615) I, p. 128.

gallia.[57] Yet the tendency to see the ancient council as a meeting of the whole community was inherent in the whole tradition. There are traces of this notion in Gaguin, and we have already noted that the Parlement was sometimes regarded as a substitute for the Estates or the people as a whole.[58]

Du Haillan, of course, was not suggesting that there was any act of legislation for which consent of the Estates was mandatory. A law was fully valid as long as the Parlement approved it. But he does suggest that the consent of the Estates was even more authoritative, and was especially appropriate where existing law was to be altered in some basic way.

Hence, looking back at the entire period from the end of the fifteenth century to 1572, we may conclude that the dominant trend of political ideas was favourable to constitutionalism. The final barrier of residual absolute authority was not yet overthrown. Yet within this limit the constitutionalist tendency was clear. The approval of the sovereign courts, if not of the Estates, was considered an essential element in every area of law and the idea of residual absolute authority was in process of gradual erosion.

This is not to say, of course, that the constitutionalist trend was universal. At every stage in the period considered, absolutist formulations can be found. Yet these were comparatively rare, and curiously passive. As we have already indicated, they did not challenge the constitutionalist trend, but rather passed it by. More deliberate absolutism came mainly from the kings themselves, or rather from certain of the chancellors. Duprat, under Francis I, had bitterly contested the right of the Parlements to continue with their remonstrations in the face of a *lettre de jussion*. L'Hôpital had taken a broadly similar position in the 1560s; and in the Edict of Moulins of 1566, which was passed with many objections, the right to remonstrate was declared to be purely advisory. And in a celebrated address to the Estates of Orleans in 1560, L'Hôpital had informed the deputies that their function was simply to advise.[59]

Yet such ideas were not systematically developed. They appeared from time to time in the course of some particular effort by the government to push its program through. If L'Hôpital denied any right in the Estates, it was largely because he had used this reassurance to persuade the queen mother and the princes to convoke them. If he denied protracted remonstrations, it was largely to hasten approval of the Ordinance which had issued from the Estates of Orleans. His ' absolutism ', therefore, need not have been very deeply held. It is even possible that, chastened by the disappointment of his hopes that the

---

[57] André Lemaire, *Les lois fondamentales de la monarchie française d'après les théoriciens de l'ancien régime* (Paris, 1907) pp. 101–2. The key point for Lemaire is Du Haillan's acceptance of the thesis of original election. But this does not concern us in this chapter. For other changes in Du Haillan's views after 1572, see Church, *Constitutional Thought*, pp. 208ff. On the *Francogallia*, see below, pp. 44–6.

[58] See p. 11 above and p. 16, n. 42.

[59] For brief discussions of L'Hôpital's constitutional views, see De Caprariis, *Propaganda e pensiero politico*, pp. 192ff, and Lemaire, *Lois fondamentales*, pp. 78ff.

kings would undertake reforms, he subsequently changed his mind. According to one source, he later conceded to the Parlement that he had been wrong in 1560.[60]

The idea of limitations would thus appear to be the dominant opinion of the decade after 1560, and an opinion that was deeply rooted in the French tradition. It is in the light of this consensus that Bodin's early work must be interpreted.

[60] Thus remonstrations of the Parlement presented to Henri III in January 1580 and claiming the right of protracted remonstrations despite a *lettre de jussion* claim that L'Hôpital (by then deceased) had openly confessed to the Court his error in supporting restrictions on the right of remonstration. Maugis, *Histoire du Parlement*, 1, pp. 620–1.

CHAPTER 2

Bodin's Early Theory of Sovereignty

Bodin's principle of sovereignty, as finally stated in the *République*, is the assertion that there must exist, in every ordered commonwealth, a single center of supreme authority and that this authority must necessarily be absolute. This proposition is presented as an analytic truth. By the very concept of a political order, a sovereign authority exists and must be absolute as well as indivisible.

But in an earlier work, Bodin presents the principle of sovereignty without the absolutist element, and this difference cannot be attributed to immaturity or inadvertence. The *Methodus ad facilem historiarum cognitionem* appeared in 1566, when Bodin was in his middle thirties, and was the fruit of some fifteen years of scholarly research in comparative history and jurisprudence. The purpose of the work was to provide the student or amateur of history with a critical and theoretical apparatus for reading historians with profit. One of the most important requirements, in Bodin's judgment, was to understand the nature of the state, the different types of states, the general causes of constitutional change, and the constitutions and changes of the most important political systems of the present and the past. Chapter VI of the *Methodus*, in which these themes are taken up, accounts for more than one-third of the bulk of the entire work and is really a treatise in itself. In the first part of this book within a book, which is very densely written, the principle of sovereignty and the doctrine of its indivisibility are stated and elaborately defended.

The thought of chapter VI of the *Methodus* is thus a mature and reasoned conception of the state, and in this early statement, absolutist elements are not only absent but are deliberately repudiated. Limited supremacy, subject to law and procedures of consent, is not only admitted as a proper form of sovereignty, but is described and recommended as the normal form of monarchy in Europe. The conception of the French kingship is a continuation and enthusiastic endorsement of the intellectual trend that we have seen in the preceding chapter. It is mistaken, therefore, to assume that the equation of supreme with absolute authority was an inherent or guiding component of Bodin's original inquiry. The absolutism of the *République* was something superadded, and in order to evaluate this change we must first understand the earlier conception.

Bodin's concern with the characteristics of supreme authority seems to have derived from very early studies on the inalienability of sovereignty in Roman law. The generally accepted rule that sovereignty could not be alienated had been ambiguous in medieval jurisprudence. In principle at least, the only valid exceptions to the rule were grants of authority and privilege that did not seriously impair the basic set of powers which each incumbent ruler was bound to pass on to his successor. But the actual application of this rule was loose. In order to account for the decentralized organization of the medieval Empire, the legal commentators had devised all manner of ingenious formulae by which they could acknowledge almost any alienation or prescription of the Emperor's authority while still maintaining that imperial unity was somehow unimpaired.[1]

The French civilians of the sixteenth century, who were thinking of the king of France and not the German Emperor, had been far less permissive on the prescription of sovereign prerogatives; they had been encouraged in this point of view by new interpretations of the Roman sources developed by the academic jurists. Beginning with the Italian commentator, Andrea Alciato, the new school of humanist civilians had shown convincingly that medieval views on alienation were often inconsistent with classic Roman usage.[2] By the 1550s, when Bodin was a student and young teacher at the law school of Toulouse, the entire doctrine was in process of revision.

The questions posed were commonly taken up in the course of commentaries on titles of the *Digest* and the *Code* which dealt with the authority and jurisdiction of magistrates. The technical problem was to define the kinds of powers held by the different sorts of magistrates. But to decide the powers that a magistrate might have was to take a position on the rights of sovereigns, at least by implication.[3] The powers inseparable from sovereignty were all those powers that a magistrate could never hold, or which he could legally exercise only by a specific and revocable grant. Bodin's earliest efforts as a legal theorist were almost surely intended as a contribution to this literature. Sometime in the 1550s he composed a monograph, or pair of monographs, entitled *De imperio et jurisdictione*. The manuscript, unpublished in his lifetime, was burned at his request upon his death. But the title indicates a treatise on the

---

[1] For the adjustment of the idea of imperial sovereignty to the federal structure of the Empire, see Cecil N. Sidney Woolf, *Bartolus of Sassoferrato* (Cambridge, 1913). The counter-trends are developed in Peter N. Riesenberg, *The Inalienability of Sovereignty in Medieval Political Thought* (New York, 1956).

[2] The most dramatic issue was the right of magistrates to ' hold ' the *merum imperium*, or ' power of the sword ', in permanent possession as a kind of usufruct. For an historical survey of this celebrated controversy, which goes back to an alleged debate between Lothair and Azo in the thirteenth century, see Myron P. Gilmore, *Argument from Roman Law in Political Thought : 1200–1600* (Cambridge, Mass., 1941). For Alciato's revolutionary attack on the dominant view that the high powers of *merum imperium* could be ' had ' by magistrates, see his *Paradoxa* (1518) in Andrea Alciato, *Opera* (Basel, 1582) IV, cols 29ff.

[3] One good example of the easy movement from one question to the other is Jean Gillot, *De jurisdictione et imperio* (1537) in *Tractatus universi juris* (Venice, 1584–6) III. See also Alciato, *Paradoxa*, vol. IV, col. 39, and Gilmore, *Argument from Roman Law*, ch. 2 *passim*.

law of magistracies, a surmise fully confirmed by allusions to the contents given by Bodin in the *Methodus*.[4]

These allusions also indicate that Bodin had already been led to general reflections on the character of sovereignty. His attempt to discover which prerogatives of government a ruler could not give away posed a question that was not directly answered by the legal texts. Since the *Corpus Juris* does not provide a list of sovereign prerogatives, it was almost useless for the purpose. The medievals had supplied this lack by incorporating the list of regalian privileges which had been claimed by Frederick I at the Diet of Roncaglia in 1158 and ratified by the Italian cities. But this was a list of feudal privileges unsuited to contemporary needs. For similar reasons French domestic custom was also unsuggestive. Here again there was no list of imprescriptible prerogatives, and most of the disputed points of law had to do with feudal rights of justice and taxation.

Bodin's contribution was to put the question of sovereign prerogatives in a more comprehensive way than anyone before him. He now attempted to derive the contents of supreme authority from the concept of supremacy itself. The question that he asked, in other words, was what prerogatives must be held by a political authority in order to say that it does not acknowledge a superior or equal in its territory.

The scope of this investigation was also affected by a crucial methodological decision. In the course of his Toulousan period, Bodin concluded that points of legal theory could not be settled by appeal to Roman norms alone. The use of philological techniques by the great French school of legal humanism had prepared the way for a methodological revolution in which Bodin became a leading figure. The more the humanists attempted to find the original meaning of the Roman texts, and to discern the underlying system of the *Corpus Juris,* the more they became critical of Roman law itself. The *Corpus Juris,* to list their main complaints,[5] seemed incomplete in many areas, and most especially in public law; Justinian and his compilers had often been cryptic and inaccurate in representing the best of Roman legal thought; many rules, some of

---

[4] *Methodus ad facilem historiarum cognitionem* (1566), Pierre Mesnard, ed., *Oeuvres philosophiques de Jean Bodin* (Paris, 1951) pp. 173, 175, 176. The first and third references are to a manuscript entitled *De imperio*. The second reference, which does not appear in the first edition, is to a work entitled *De jure imperio* [sic]. This would appear to be a mistaken rendition either of *De jure imperii*, or, more probably, of *De jurisdictione*. The latter title is much more appropriate to the context in which the citation appears, and it is mentioned along with *De imperio*, in a list of five manuscripts – all having titles suggestive of technical legal studies – that Bodin ordered to be burned at his death. The authority for this is Aegidius Menagius (Ménage), *Vita Petri Aerodii*, p. 143, cited in Roger Chauviré, *Jean Bodin, auteur de la République* (La Flèche, 1914) p. 95. Beatrice Reynolds also suggests *De jurisdictione* in her translation of the *Methodus*, *Method for the Easy Comprehension of History* (New York, 1945) p. 173, n. 52.

[5] For a survey of this anti-Romanist trend in humanist legal thought, see Julian H. Franklin, *Jean Bodin and the Sixteenth Century Revolution in the Methodology of Law and History* (New York, 1963) ch. III.

them basic to the system, were peculiar to the Roman state and obsolete for France; the *Corpus Juris* had not been arranged into a logically coherent system, and could not be because of its defects and omissions.[6]

One consequence of this critique was to strengthen that emphasis on domestic legal custom to which we alluded in the previous chapter. An additional motif, especially characteristic of Bodin, was the idea of remedying deficiences in Roman law by consulting the materials of universal history.[7] This, according to Bodin, was the only way to construct a truly universal legal science: to compare ' all the laws of all, or the most famous, states and to select the best variety '.[8]

Some years earlier, a grandiose design for this comparison had been projected in his *Juris universi distributio*, or *Sketch of Law in its Entirety*; and the sixth chapter of the *Methodus* of 1566 was a preliminary statement of his findings in the area of public law. In this fashion an inquiry originally focused on the special prerogatives of the king of France and the Emperor of ancient Rome was thus transformed into a study of sovereignty in every kind of state.

It is at this point, I would suggest, that Bodin was lured to the idea that sovereignty is indivisible. The premise in chapter VI of the *Methodus*, and throughout his examination of public law, is that sovereign authority has several forms, and is to be found not only in monarchies but also in republics. Bodin assumed, in other words, that the ' Senate ' in an aristocracy or the assembly of the people in a democracy had the same status with respect to other components of the commonwealth as that of the ruler in a monarchy.

But this equation is either mistaken or dangerously misleading. The idea of sovereignty is monarchical in connotation. It immediately suggests the ' sway ' or ' dominion ' of one person over others, the first ruling and the others being ruled. But in a pure democracy this relationship of ruler and subject does not obtain in any obvious or determinate sense. The entire society, as it were, is included in the ' subject ' of sovereignty. *Mutatis mutandis*, the same ' peculiarity ' applies to aristocracies as well.

The identification of the nobles or the people as ' the sovereign persons ' of republics is thus legitimate only by a legal fiction. If the nobles or the people are construed as a *persona ficta* or *moralis*, the procedures of decision-making can be cast into a ' royal ' form. The *persona ficta* can then be taken as the ruler of the general society, i.e., of all its parts in their individual capacities.

---

[6] All these themes are briefly mentioned by Bodin in the dedicatory epistle to the *Methodus*. The most elaborate critique is Hotman's *Antitribonian*, written one year later but not published until 1603.

[7] Thus Hotman, *Antitribonianus*, in *Variorum opuscula ad cultiorem jurisprudentiam adsequendam pertinentia* (Pisa, 1771), vol. VII, pp. 140ff and also François Baudouin, *De institutione historiae universae et ejus cum jurisprudentia conjunctione* Προλεγόμενων (1561) (Halle, 1726) p. 29.

[8] *Methodus*, Dedicatory epistle, Mesnard ed., p. 107 (2). Much the same thought is also expressed in the Dedicatory epistle to his *Juris universi distributio*, Pierre Mesnard ed., *Oeuvres philosophiques de Jean Bodin* (Paris, 1951), p. 71, which almost surely dates from his Toulousan period.

Bodin, however, moved from monarchical to other forms of state without examining this intervening step. Given the conventions of the time, his inadvertence was natural enough. In the tradition stemming from the ancients, the nobles or the people had always been treated as substantial entities. The people, for example, were most often envisaged as the ' poor ', and thus as one part of the society which ruled the rest in a democracy. Bodin, accordingly could look upon the nobles or the people as if they were a person, without observing that a legal fiction was implied.

For most purposes this omission was a purely technical defect that did not affect the substance of his argument. But one far-reaching consequence was Bodin's inability to comprehend the notion of a mixed constitution in the sense of a sovereign authority shared among the people, the nobles, and the king. From the standpoint of a theory of sovereignty, ' the sovereign ' of a mixed constitution would have to be described as a *persona ficta* composed of all three parts, with each part, or the members of each part, sharing in the making of ' the sovereign's ' decisions. This solution would soon be pointed out by Christopher Besold, who was one of the shrewdest of Bodin's early critics.[9]

But Bodin, having no theoretical conception of a corporate or fictive sovereign, was simply unable to imagine this. He was always thinking of ' the sovereign ' as one part of the society that rules the rest, according to the familiar model of a kingship. It seemed to follow, therefore, that if all three parts should share in sovereignty the entire relation of ruler and subject would evaporate, along with the state and sovereignty itself. That the outcome would be the same in a complete democracy, where all the people rule, escaped his notice utterly. The problem of division was always considered from the standpoint of a king, or as though the people or the nobles had the posture of a king.

The sharing of sovereignty could thus appear as a logical absurdity. By negating the relation of subjection, it seemed a negation of the state itself. Or to put it in another way, a mixed constitution seemed a contradiction in the

---

[9] *De majestate in genere ejusque juribus specialibus . . . accedit tractatio singularis de reipublicae statu mixto* (1618) in Christopher Besold, *Operis politici, editio nova* (Strasbourg, 1626) pp. 212ff. Besold is answering Daniel Ottho, who had attacked Besold and Bartholomaeus Keckermann for having defected from Bodin's position. Besold briefly summarizes and replies to seven arguments for indivisibility. His diagnosis of the error contained in all of them seems to be suggested in his reply to the first argument: ' It is never possible, he [Ottho] says, either in nature or even in imagination for supreme authority or majesty to be mixed with an inferior and still remain supreme. It remains supreme, I answer, but not in one individual. It is rather in the whole body or corporation (*collegio*) of those who rule (*archonton*) but in such a way that it is not distributed equally among the parts. The prince will be conceded some large degree of eminence (which will be larger, of course, than what the Doge has in the Venetian commonwealth) or else it will be an aristocracy ' (p. 212). A few sentences earlier Besold makes the decisive point that a mixed state is no less comprehensible than a simple aristocracy or democracy. ' As in a simple polyarchic state, majesty properly and integrally resides in that entire body which participates in majesty.'

adjective. A constitution is a ' state ' or ' condition ' of the sovereign authority. But a mixed constitution is a negation of authority as such, and thus a ' state ' of anarchy.

The fallacy in all of this is so transparent to the modern reader, and so profoundly foreign, that it is sometimes tempting to look for deeper lines of reasoning. For Bodin, on the other hand, the argument for indivisibility seemed so self-evident that he was hardly able to articulate his grounds. There is little argument at all in the *Methodus*, and the arguments later offered in the *République* involve such gross non-sequiturs that the modern reader often fails to see any connection whatsoever between premise and conclusion.

Thus one of Bodin's favourite arguments for indivisibility is based on the very simple observation that if a sovereign prince should share his power with a subject, he would no longer have the status of a sovereign:

Thus all [the jurists] agree that royal rights cannot be ceded, are inalienable, and cannot be prescribed by any tract of time. If a sovereign prince should share them with a subject, he makes a companion of his servitor, and in so doing is no longer sovereign. For the term sovereign, which refers to one who is above all subjects, cannot apply to someone who has made a companion of his servitor . . . The prince . . . cannot make a subject equal to himself without negating his own power.[10]

From a modern standpoint, the truth of this seems trite. Where sovereignty is shared by more than one, it cannot belong to one alone. But for Bodin the implications seemed momentous. For one thing, he seems to have thought that a king who would share his authority with others is no longer ' king ' in any sense at all, since he does not rule alone. Monarchy, accordingly, could not be mixed with other forms, for in the very act of mixture the monarchical element – or rule of one – would disappear! The further implication, virtually inarticulate, is that rule itself would disappear. If the king, in sharing power with his subjects, does not divest himself of all of it, there will be no highest power, and no authority at all!

Bodin, however, is sometimes more articulate, and comes very close to a clear expression of the fallacy in the following passage on the indivisibility of legislative power:

For if sovereignty is indivisible, as we have shown, how could it be shared by a prince, the nobles, and the people at the same time? The first mark of sovereignty is to give the law to subjects, and where then will be the subjects who obey, if they also have the power to make law? And what individual can give the law, if he is himself constrained to take it from those to whom he gives it? The conclusion follows necessarily, that, if no one in particular has the power to make law, and this power belongs to all together, the commonwealth is democratic.[11]

---

[10] *Les six livres de la république* (1576) (Paris, 1583; reprinted by Scientia Verlag, Aalen, Germany, 1961) I, 10, 215 (155).
[11] *Ibid.* pp. 254–5 (185).

The last sentence, in which the outcome of division is described, was to undergo an illuminating change in the Latin edition of 1586.[12] In the later version the outcome is described as anarchy, which was, no doubt, a better rendition of Bodin's underlying thought. But the closeness, in his mind, of democracy and anarchy nicely reveals the ultimate confusion. A regime in which all components participate in the making of decisions cannot be distinguished from anarchy, because it no longer displays the subjection of society to a natural person. Having no conception of a corporate sovereign, Bodin was ultimately unable to draw any stable distinction between a mixed constitution and democracy, and between either one of these and anarchy.[13]

Up to here we have been speaking of mixture or division only in the sense of sharing. From a modern standpoint the most obvious example would be the sharing of legislative power by two or more components of a compound legislature. But Bodin was also concerned to deny the possibility of distribution. This, from a modern standpoint, would be the separation of governmental functions, as when the executive or judicial power is divided from the legislative by being placed in separate hands. Although this position is not of immediate importance for Bodin's interpretation of French institutions, it is so interwoven with his other views on indivisibility that some examination of his thinking seems desirable.

The modern idea of separated powers depends on the rather subtle, and at first sight curious, thought that executive power can be simultaneously independent and subordinate. The subordination of executive to legislative is indispensable to the coordination of the legal system. But this subordination is not achieved through direct control by the legislative power. It depends on the fact that executive power stands to the legislative in the relationship of means to end. It is subordinated to the latter by the inherent nature of its function. Its independence, therefore, means that the legislative power is also restricted by its function. The legislative must be constitutionally forbidden to assume the role of the executive – either by direct expropriation of executive functions or by the issuance of particular decrees.

But the idea of fixed jurisdictional relationships was beyond Bodin's theoretical resources. When he thought of separated powers, he assumed that one or

---

[12] *De republica libri sex* (Paris, 1586) II, 1, p. 176.
[13] The tendency to identify monarchy with the essence of ' rule ' as such is nicely illustrated by Bartholomaeus Keckermann, *Systema disciplinae politicae* (Hanover, 1607) p. 33: Monarchy is the simplest of political regimes because its essence is unity (*quia in unitate consistit*) and because it reduces the multitude of subjects to unity of a natural sort (*ad naturalem unitatem*).' This statement is particularly revealing because Keckermann is not an absolutist. He admits a right of resistance to any form of state, and he seems to prefer a mixed monarchy. Yet he is unable to comprehend division of sovereignty, and tried to accommodate the mixed constitution by applying Bodin's distinction between the form of government and the form of state. The result is a misinterpretation of Bodin and general confusion of the issue. See p. 560.

more of them must be inherently entitled to annex the jurisdictions of the rest. In the *Methodus* this control of jurisdictions may well have seemed inherent in the 'executive' power of 'creating magistrates and assigning each one's duties', which was then regarded as the 'first and most important mark of sovereignty'.[14] But no explanation was as yet attempted. Later on, in the *République*, the power to control all other jurisdictions seemed to be an inherent and inevitable aspect of the legislative power, and it is also discovered in the power of receiving oaths of fealty, which had now been added as a right of majesty. Both of these powers, therefore, would not only be in conflict with each other in a scheme of separated powers, but each would be in conflict with all others:

> But, someone will say, can there not be a commonwealth in which the people create the officers, dispose of revenues, and grant pardons – which are three marks of sovereignty; and in which the nobility makes the laws, orders peace or war, and levies direct and indirect taxation – which are also marks of sovereignty; and in which there is, in addition, a royal magistrate above all others to whom the people as a whole and each person in particular renders faith and liege homage, and who judges in last resort without avenue of appeal or civil request? Would this not be to compose a commonwealth which is at once aristocratic, royal, and popular? I answer that no state like this was ever found, and that none can be made or even be imagined, seeing that the marks of sovereignty are indivisible. For he who will have the power to make law for all, that is to say, the power of commanding or forbidding what he pleases without any one being able to appeal from his commands or even to oppose them, he [I say] will forbid the others to make either war or peace, to levy taxes, or to render faith and homage without his leave. And he to whom fealty and liege homage are due, will obligate the nobility and the people to render obedience to no one but himself. And so will it always have to come to arms, until such time as sovereignty resides in the prince, in the lesser part of the people, or in all the people.[15]

In this passage the power to make law is considered to be absolute, which is in line with Bodin's later concept of supremacy. But I do not believe that the argument depends on this primarily. The obstacle to separated power is not located in the right of the legislative to make any decision that it wishes with respect to private persons, or subjects generally. It is found rather in its power to make laws affecting the rights of other jurisdictions.

Bodin, we may note incidentally, was also persuaded that every prerogative of sovereignty – like, for example, the right of hearing final appeals in civil and criminal cases – was somehow 'contained' in the power to make law, and that possession of the latter implied a claim to all the rest.[16] But his thoughts on this

---

14 See below, p. 32.

15 *République*, p. 266 (193–4).

16 *Ibid.* pp. 223–4 (161–2). The absence of clear theoretical classification of governmental powers is characteristic of the tradition.

proposition, which may have influenced his doctrine of inseparability, are even less illuminating than the one that we have just described. The ultimate unity of powers is made to depend upon the fact that almost every governmental act involves the power of issuing a binding command. Since the legislative power is defined, in this context, as the power of issuing commands of every type, it is simply an abstract name for political authority in general. The functional differences between different sorts of power are simply ignored.

Once again, it might be tempting for a modern reader to look for something more. But here, too, the criticism of a near-contemporary may help to reassure us on that score. Early critics, like Besold and Henning Arnisaeus, generally accept the view that all governmental functions, in their highest aspects, are the ' parts ' of a power to command. They do not have a definite conception of functional relationships. But they do maintain that a corporate sovereign is possible if the parts of sovereignty are distributed in such a way that the rights of each component are restricted by the functions of the others. For this reason, Arnisaeus, who accepts Bodin's position on the impossibility of sharing sovereignty, will not go along with his doctrine of inseparability:

He [Bodin] concedes rights to the particular components such as carry with them the entirety of majesty, and this may not be done as we said a little while ago. Thus the power to make law on all topics cannot be given to some one component because power over everything goes with it. Nor can subjects be obligated to the king in all respects in this mixed commonwealth, because to do this is to lay the supreme power in the king's lap.[17]

Although Bodin's position on the ' mixed constitution ' seems naive from a modern point of view, it was natural and almost unavoidable at the time he actually wrote. In the sixteenth century, there were simply no materials that directly pointed to another view. Much had been said in Bodin's time about the advantages of a mixed constitution. But when he turned to the historical materials, he was unable to discover any clear example of divided sovereignty, or even any clear suggestion of what separation or division might entail.

In the humanist tradition the best-known example of the ' mixed constitution ' was the Roman Republic of classical antiquity. Because of Polybius and a whole host of later writers who elaborated on his point of view, it was the only constitution, traditionally reputed mixed, on which Bodin and his contemporaries were reasonably well informed. Ancient Athens was not regarded as a mixed constitution; Lycurgan Sparta was not known in significant detail; and the actual procedures of contemporary Venice were difficult to penetrate and were often represented in accordance with the Roman model.

Rome, then, was the crucial case. Yet the Roman constitution of Polybius' time was not a mixture, at least in strictest law, and Bodin was the first to

---

[17] Henning Arnisaeus, *Doctrina politica in genuinam methodum quae est Aristotelis reducta* (1606) in *Opera politica omnia* (Strasbourg, 1648) 1, p. 66.

see this clearly. In passage after passage, Polybius himself, and all the other commentators, had regularly attributed powers to the Roman people which amounted to juridical supremacy. Bodin could therefore see that on Polybius' own account, the position of the Roman people was legally analogous to the status of the king of France or the ancient Roman Emperor. The Roman constitution, therefore, was best represented as a ' pure democracy '; and Bodin was able to conclude, triumphantly, that Polybius and all the other ancients had been wrong in speaking of a mixture.

In one respect this criticism was ungenerous. When Polybius and the others spoke of mixture, they were not attempting to describe the basic juridical relationships of the Roman constitution, but the actual balance of effective political influence. To this extent, Bodin was misreading their usage of the term. Yet in the larger sense his own interpretation was superior in being more precise. He was perfectly willing to admit that the Roman Senate had exercised considerable influence, and this influence, he thought, had been highly beneficial to the Roman system.[18] But he was broadly right in holding that all the powers of the Senate were technically held on revocable delegation or sufferance of the people.[19] From a strictly legal standpoint, therefore, the Roman republic was a pure democracy.[20]

Thus the Roman constitution, ironically enough, was a confirmation of Bodin's position rather than a serious refutation. And the irony has many aspects. It is very likely that Bodin was led to formulate his principle of indivisibility by reflections on the Roman constitution, for he had no reason to make the point at all, except to rebut the traditional opinion. It is also very likely that his first formulation of the rights of sovereignty was directly suggested by none other than Polybius. In presenting his list of 1566, Bodin virtually announces this:

And so, having compared the arguments of Aristotle, Polybius, Dionysius [of Halicarnassus], and the jurists – with each other and with the universal history of public affairs – I find that supremacy in a commonwealth consists of five parts. The first and most important is creating magistrates and assigning each one's duties; another is ordaining and repealing laws; a third is declaring and terminating war; a fourth is the right of hearing appeals from all magistrates in last resort; and the last is the power of life and death where the law itself has made no provision for flexibility or clemency.[21]

Indeed, on close inspection, it turns out that this list was probably drawn up with a passage from Polybius in mind which must have been highly suggestive to Bodin as to the nature of the Roman constitution, since it purported to describe the powers of the Roman people. According to Polybius,

---

[18] *Methodus*, p. 179 (183). [19] *Ibid*. p. 179 (184).
[20] *Ibid*. p. 177 (179): ' I therefore hold that the Roman state was surely popular in Polybius' time, and even more so in the time of Dionysius and Cicero '.
[21] *Ibid*. pp. 174–5 (172–3).

there is a part and a very important part left for the people. For it is the people which alone has the right to confer honors and inflict punishment ... [And] they are the only court that may try on capital charges ... Again it is the people who bestow office on the deserving, the noblest reward of virtue in a state; the people have the power of approving and rejecting laws: and what is most important of all, they deliberate on the question of war or peace.[22]

Bodin, studying this passage, could have hardly failed to note that the powers of the popular assembly, in the classical account of a mixed constitution, were the very powers required for supremacy.

There were of course certain periods of Roman history to which the idea of the republic as a pure democracy did not apply exactly. Prior to the third century B.C., and even later on occasion, the Senate still contended for its ancient privilege of authorizing legislation by the people. But the constitutional basis of this claim, and the legal effect of authorization, were unclear in Bodin's time; and there was similar obscurity surrounding analogous functions in the Senate of Lycurgan Sparta and the inner councils of contemporary Venice. Bodin could thus ignore the implications of a veto power in these bodies. He seems to have thought that their right of authorization was essentially advisory. In this respect at least, the functions of republican ' senates ' seemed to be much the same as those of a royal privy council.[23]

Hence, for all Bodin could see, there were no republican arrangements that contradicted the unity of sovereignty. Exceptions to the rule would later be collected by his early critics.[24] But I do not believe that he would have altered his opinion, even had he known of these. His confusion on indivisibility was so deeply rooted that nothing but a deliberate and eminently successful example to the contrary could have led him to perceive his error. His later sympathizers would dismiss all minor exceptions as ' impurities ', and deliberate exceptions as rare and monstrous abnormalities.[25] In the *République* such lines of defense are already anticipated.

[22] Polybius, *Histories*, W. R. Paton, trans., Loeb Classical Library (London 1923) III, pp. 301–3.

[23] *Methodus*, pp. 177–8 (180): ' Where then is the supposed aristocracy of Senators? If there is any, then it must exist in kingdoms also, since the council constituted by the prince has the same power (*parem potestatem*) as the Roman Senate. But to associate the council with the prince in power is not only foolish, but even a capital crime. The same is to be said about the Roman Senate, to which those writers give a share of power with the people, and thus associate the master of a state in partnership with his servants and agents.' But cf. *ibid.* p. 183 (194) where different degrees of power in senates are recognized and the issue of a veto is only barely avoided.

[24] Among the earliest critics was the French juridical humanist Vincent Cabot, whose demonstration of mixture in pre-Polybian phases of the Roman constitution was especially decisive and seems to have been highly influential for subsequent critics, most of whom were German. See Vincent Cabot, *Variarum juris publici et privati disputationum libri duo* (1598) in Gerard Meerman, ed., *Novus thesaurus juris civilis et canonici* (The Hague, 1751–3) IV, pp. 662–3.

[25] Among earlier writers, critical as well as friendly, the ' impurities ' of a constitution were not decisive for its classification so long as one of three components of the polity ' pre-

Bodin, finally, was fully persuaded that the principle of indivisibility was in no way incompatible with the French constitution as traditionally conceived.[26] In 1566, at least, he was not aware of any contradiction between the sovereign status of a king and the kinds of limitations upon royal power which we have described in the preceding chapter. Seyssel, reflecting on this scheme of limitations, had once declared that the French system 'participates in all three modes of political government',[27] a notion that was guardedly taken over by Pasquier.[28] But the figure of mixture had never been intended literally as a legal division of supreme authority. Du Haillan, perhaps reacting to Bodin's disapproval of the figure, would soon be very careful to point out that it must not be taken as a denial of unitary sovereignty. The kings, he says,

of their own motion have established laws and officers by whose power and authority they [the kings] have voluntarily restrained and bridled their power, which is not on that account demeaned, diminished, or debased in any way. It has, on the contrary, been rendered more secure and ample, and more willingly supported. We do not say that France is a state composed of three modes of government, or that it is divided into three absolute and equal powers, each one in possession of its own authority. We say only that it seems to be so . . . [and] there is a great difference between seeming and being.[29]

Hence Du Haillan, and presumably the other constitutionalists, did not think of institutional restraints as parts of sovereign authority. Limitations were intuitively regarded as checks external to sovereign authority, designed to keep it within proper bounds. From this perspective the constitutionalists felt able to maintain that the king of France was sovereign, and even absolute, while still insisting upon limitations.

With Bodin, of course, even the most figurative reference to a mixed constitution was suppressed.[30] The principle of mixture could properly apply to

ponderated '. Thus Cabot, *Variarum juris*, p. 623; Arnisaeus, *Doctrina politica*, p. 64; Besold, *De majestate*, p. 211; and Johannes Althusius, *Politica methodice digesta* (1603) (Cambridge, Mass., 1932) p. 405. Samuel Pufendorf, *On the Law of Nature and Nations* (1672) (1688 edition, C. H. and W. A. Oldfather, trans., Oxford, 1934) pp. 1040ff, discerns a whole class of deliberately 'irregular' states held together by fragile comity among the parts rather than by any unifying legal principle. Cf. *République*, pp. 266–7 (194) and especially pp. 270–1 (198).

[26] The constitutionalism of the *Methodus* is sometimes understated as in Chauviré, *Jean Bodin*, pp. 271ff and De Caprariis, *Propaganda e pensiero politico*, pp. 362–3. The former regards it as a minor variation from the absolutism of the *République*, the latter as a mere gesture to traditional ideas. More accurate, in my opinion, are Beatrice Reynolds, *Proponents of Limited Monarchy in Sixteenth Century France : Francis Hotman and Jean Bodin* (New York, 1931) pp. 123–4; John L. Brown, *The Methodus ad Facilem Historiarum Cognitionem, A Critical Study* (Washington, D.C., 1939) pp. 120ff; and especially Jean Moreau-Reibel, *Jean Bodin et le droit public comparé dans ses rapports avec la philosophie de l'histoire* (Paris, 1933) pp. 66ff.

[27] Seyssel, *Prohème*, p. 80.

[28] *Recherches*, p. 56.   [29] *De l'estat et succez*, 156v.

[30] In *Methodus*, p. 177 (180), the thought is repudiated as not only 'foolish, but a capital crime '.

the mode in which authority is exercised, or what Bodin called the form of government. But it has no application to the form of state, or basic constitution which is the mode in which authority is ' owned '.[31] Yet even so, he felt fully able to assimilate the idea of binding limitations. Indeed, in some respects, Bodin's expression of this principle was even bolder than those we have previously considered. Dealing, as he was, with sovereignty in general, he was naturally led to resolve the issue more abstractly.

Almost at the beginning of his discussion of the types of monarchy, Bodin inquires whether it is possible and proper for a sovereign ruler to be subject to the law. He begins his answer negatively. There is perhaps a sense in which a sovereign must be superior to law in order to adapt it to a change in circumstances. But this conclusion is immediately qualified. A sovereign's superiority to law does not necessarily or properly imply that he is free to change it at his own discretion :

It is an honest way of speaking to hold, for the reasons we have given, that he who gives the law must be above the laws. But once the law is passed, and has been fully approved by the consent of all, why should the prince not be bound by the law he has established? This is the reason why the *Lex Cornelia Tribunitia* was adopted, which provided that praetors should be obligated by their edicts, and that a praetor could neither change nor abrogate his edict once it had been set [at the beginning of his term]. For as Asconius writes, it had been the custom of the praetors, arrogantly and at their own discretion, to issue decrees in conflict with their edicts. But the relation of a praetor to an edict is the same as that of a prince or a people to the law. Hence if it is only fair that he who makes a law for others should be bound by it himself, is it not even fairer that the prince or the people should be obligated by their own laws?

This is why the Roman people used to swear to a law that they had passed...

Since, therefore, the people was bound by its law until abrogation was more equitable, it follows that princes too are bound. Princes speak sophistically against the people when they say that their freedom from the law is so complete that they are not only above the laws, but are not obliged in any way, or, even more disgracefully, that what has pleased them has the force of law.[32]

The basic import of this argument is that a king's superiority to law is properly restricted to those occasions on which he has the consent of the community to change it. Since the ultimate sanction for an act of legislation is the general consent of the community, when that consent has been accomplished, the king is subject to his own enactments. In this sense a proper sovereign is supreme and limited at once.

There is, however, one hint of an exception to this principle for which some interpretation is required. Alluding to the Roman people, Bodin says that it was bound to the laws which it had passed only so long as they continued to

---

[31] *Ibid.* p. 168 (156). The distinction, only mentioned here, is elaborated at several points in the *République*, among which see especially II, 2, p. 272 (199–200).

[32] *Methodus*, p. 187 (203).

be equitable. By implication the grounds for abrogation could be determined by the people unilaterally, which might suggest that a king should be similarly empowered.

But it will soon be clear, from other things that Bodin says, that he did not intend this exception to be generalized. He is simply recognizing, half-confusedly, that in strictly democratic commonwealths the usual relationships of obligation are logically excluded by the nature of the sovereign. Where the sovereign body encompasses the whole community, the community does not appear as an independent entity which receives and ratifies the sovereign's enactments. This peculiarity of democratic commonwealths is elaborated in the *République*, and we may infer that Bodin was aware of it in 1566. In the later work, where he is speaking of absolute authority, he contends that the legislative power of a proper sovereign may never be restricted by a promise made to the community. He then points out that the absurdity of any such engagement is most clearly illustrated by the characteristics of a democratic sovereign:

If, then, it is useful that a sovereign prince, to govern well, should have the legislative power all to himself, it is even more expedient for the ruler in an aristocracy, and absolutely necessary for the people in a democratic state. For the monarch is distinguished from the people, and in an aristocratic state the nobles are distinguished from the common people, so that in both commonwealths there are two parties: one that holds the sovereignty on the one hand, and the people on the other. Hence the contentions arising between them on the rights of sovereignty, which are abeyant in a popular state. For if the prince or the nobles who hold the state are obliged to keep the laws, as some people think, and can make no law without the approval of the people or the Senate, then the law cannot be abrogated without the consent of the one body or the other, according to the rule of civil law. Nothing of this sort can occur in a popular state, because the people constitutes a single body and cannot be obligated to itself.[33]

In 1566, on the other hand, Bodin was apparently taking this peculiarity of democratic sovereigns as the exception rather than the norm. A sovereign monarch can and should be subject to the law; but a ruling people unfortunately cannot be, except by moral self-restraint. Bodin would like to hold that even democracies can tie their hands, but given his simple conception of community, he cannot see how this could be accomplished institutionally.

The main part of his discussion, however, centers on the forms of legitimate monarchy, among which two main classes are distinguished. Included in the first are all those rulers whom Aristotle had called lords or despots because they rule their subjects the way fathers rule their households, and because they hold their commonwealths as personal property. Examples of this sort are the kings of the Turks, the Persians, and the Abyssinians.

[33] *République*, 1, 8, p. 143 (99).

Although these ' despotic ' kingships may be consistent with the law of nature so long as they are justly exercised, their legitimacy is only marginal.

In Bodin's delineation of this class, however, the concept of despotic kingship is not confined to systems of ' paternal ' rule. It is also extended, significantly enough, to any ruler who lays claim to absolute authority. Included, therefore, are the primitive or ' savage ' kingships of the Scythians and Britons, and also, somewhat oddly, the contemporary Papacy since the Popes contend that they ' never tie their hands '.[34] The underlying thought, apparently, is that every sort of absolute authority, no matter what its social form, is the outgrowth or continuation of primitive rule or else a reversion to that form.

The second class of monarchies is portrayed, by contrast, as the correlate of full civility. With the passage of primitive conditions, the people or the nobles, reacting to tyrannical abuses, subjected kings to law in the course of violent struggles.[35] In European states this struggle and this outcome had been especially common because the peoples of the ' middle region ' are endowed with independent temperaments by the effects of geography and climate.[36]

The obligations of European princes, therefore, are grounded on long-established usage. But they do not depend on this alone. The rule of custom is explicitly confirmed by their oath of coronation, which is binding by the law of nature. This interpretation of the coronation oath as a universal guarantee was rather novel at the time. The coronation promise had been used to establish specific limitations like the inalienability of royal domain, and in the thought of Chasseneuz, as we have seen, it was closely associated with the confirmation of provincial customs. With Bodin, however, who admires Chasseneuz and may be pursuing his idea, the coronation promise goes to the basic legal order as a whole:

[W]hen they are inaugurated in the rites of coronation they swear a mighty oath in a form prescribed by the priests and by the notables of the kingdom by which the kings obligate themselves to govern the commonwealth according to the fundamental laws and equity (*ex legibus imperii et aequo bono*). But the coronation formula of our kings is not only especially outstanding for its language and antiquity; it seems to me to be the fairest of them all for the weight and gravity of what is said. And in this especially: that the prince, in the presence of the priests, swears by the immortal God that he will render due law and justice (*debitam legem et*

---

[34] *Methodus*, p. 187 (204). On primitive kingships, before the time that law was instituted, see p. 186 (201).   [35] *Ibid.* p. 192 (215–16).

[36] *Ibid.* p. 192 (216–17): ' Since men of the middle region are born for the conduct of affairs, as we said in the preceding chapter, they all believe they have a claim to power, and the westerners most especially because they are more spirited than the orientals. Hence they [i.e. men of the middle region of the West] do not put up easily with tyranny. Either they compel the kings to keep the law (than which nothing more divine could be desired) or they throw the tyrants out of power and establish democratic or aristocratic states.' The influence of meridional and longitudinal situation on the ' natural temperament ' of peoples is described in chapter 5.

justitiam) to every order of society, and will judge with religion and integrity so far as in him lies. And once he has sworn he cannot easily violate his pledge, or if he could, he does not wish to. He is subject to the courts like any private individual (*jus enim illi dicitur ut privato cuique*), and he is held by the same laws. Moreover, he cannot uproot the laws proper to the kingdom as a whole, nor alter anything whatever in the practices and ancient custom of the regions without the consent of the Three Estates.[37]

This formulation is particularly bold because it uses the terminology of legal obligation. Whereas other writers of the time cautiously use the language of prediction, Bodin says the ruler ' cannot '. He is also more distinct than other commentators in saying, unequivocally, that the consent of the Estates is requisite for legislation. The only question is whether he is referring to the provincial or the general Estates. The context would suggest that he is mainly thinking of the former without intending to exclude the latter.

The preceding passage also indicates that established law is guaranteed by court review. In his elaboration of this point for France, Bodin's language is again unusually forceful:

Of all the fundamental laws of the realm none is more sacred than that which forbids any credit to the rescripts of our princes unless they are in conformity with equity and truth. On this account they are often repudiated by the magistrates, and for the same reason favors secured by importuning are of no advantage to the wicked. For the voice of the magistrates is often heard: that the prince can do nothing against the law.[38]

In this passage Bodin is referring to particular decrees. But in another and even more striking formulation, the same idea is extended to review of legislation by the sovereign courts. The passage should perhaps be quoted to illustrate the strength and direction of the trend that we described in the preceding chapter: ' The sovereign courts ', Bodin maintains,

take no account of laws unless they have approved them by their own promulgation; and they say they cannot be coerced. Yet custom, lapsing, goes astray. Would that they [the sovereign courts] would imitate the virtues of our forefathers, who would have yielded life before yielding their opinion.[39]

Thus in 1566 Bodin's idea of sovereignty was deliberately adapted to the French tradition of limited monarchy. An absolute authority might be legitimate in certain circumstances. But the civilized and proper form of sovereignty was supremacy within the law.

This notion of limited supremacy is not defined or reasoned through, and yet it was a workable conception even from the standpoint of consistency. In any legal order there is a range of discretionary powers which are anticipated by the law itself. The power of pardon and other forms of clemency are

---

[37] *Ibid.* p. 187 (204).
[38] *Ibid.* p. 208 (254).   [39] *Ibid.*

required in the interests of equity. The appointment of high executive officials, which colors administrative policy, requires some discretion in the choice of persons. The basic rules of law must be adapted to changing situations by quasi-legislative acts which, in modern terminology, are often called executive decrees. Where all of these prerogatives are vested in a single actor, it is meaningful to say that he is supreme within the limits of the law. A limited supreme authority would then be defined as one that possesses all of the discretionary powers that are normally required for the day-to-day conduct of affairs.

Along with this, however, a negative condition must be stipulated. Limited authority cannot be supreme if it is held at the pleasure of another. In Bodin's usage, the law by which the sovereign is bound cannot be changed except at his initiative, and thus with his approval. Furthermore, the review of his decisions by the courts is theoretically restricted in its scope. In principle, at least, his acts may not be disallowed unless there is clear trespass of a basic norm. Hence the complete definition of a limited supreme authority is one that is not responsible to any human agent for the use of its discretionary power, so long as it remains within the bounds of settled law, and it is this definition of supremacy that is implied by Bodin's usage.

Furthermore, the notion of limited supremacy was not so fluid and elastic as to erase the distinction between an actual ruler and a figurehead. Bodin was fully able, therefore, to distinguish princes who were truly sovereign from those whose titles were purely honorific. His main example of the latter was the status of the German Emperor. With the accumulation of restrictions, culminating in the Golden Bull, the imperial title seemed to have been voided of its original significance. Appointments by the Emperor were no longer at his own discretion but required approval by the Diet. In legislative matters, the Emperor was not only bound by the decision of the Diet, but could not prevent it from assembling, or compel it to assemble for matters he considered urgent. The Emperor, finally, could also be deposed.[40] For these and similar reasons, Bodin concluded that sovereign power had been finally transferred to the Diet, and that the German Empire was not a monarchy at all, but an aristocratic state. Like the Doge of Venice, and perhaps the kings of Denmark and Poland, the German Emperor was but the ' prince ' or first person of the commonwealth by virtue of precedence and etiquette. In the *République*, Bodin would call a system of this sort a ' principate '.[41]

---

[40] *Ibid.* pp. 188–9 (206–7).

[41] *République*, II, 5, pp. 301–2 (221). Besold, *De majestate*, p. 212, triumphantly concludes that, in admitting the category of a principate, Bodin has covertly acknowledged the possibility of mixture: ' And at certain points Bodin acknowledges principate as a kind of state intermediate between aristocracy and monarchy; and thus a form in some sort mixed.' But Besold's reading is, I think, too hasty. Some of the states that Bodin describes as principates should probably have been called mixed constitutions. But the category of principate is well-defined in principle, as for example in his comments on the Doge of Venice, *République*,

Whether this judgment was accurate or not for any particular regime is a question that need not detain us. The important point for present purposes is that Bodin, in the *Methodus*, made consistent use of a concept of limited supremacy, even though he never attempted to articulate it formally. To use Seyssel's expression, the form of sovereignty he recommended was ' neither too absolute nor too restrained '.[42] If the powers of the Turkish sultan were too complete for civil governance, the German Emperor was so restricted that he did not rule at all. The measure of a proper sovereign was thus the power of the king of France, who ruled, but ruled within the law.

Hence, despite his confusions as to indivisibility, Bodin's conception of supremacy in 1566 was flexible enough to account for the historical appearances. With the possible exception of the German Empire, where some distortion may have entered his account, his idea of undivided sovereignty was roughly adapted to all political systems as contemporaries knew and understood them. Above all it was completely adapted to the French constitutionalist tradition, which Bodin not only accepted but deliberately embraced.

I, 10, p. 219 (158). Bodin's error seems to lie less in the notion of a principate than in its application.

42 More literally, ' not totally absolute, nor yet too much restrained ', Seyssel, *Monarchie de France*, p. 115.

CHAPTER 3

The Shift to Absolutism

The absolutism of the *République*, accordingly, was not a direct and natural outgrowth of Bodin's earlier position. It was a sudden and dramatic shift which is best explained by a new political concern. It was, specifically, the outcome of his alarmed reaction to the revolutionary movement set off by the St Bartholomew's Day Massacre of 1572.

Open conflict between the state and the Calvinist reformers had been in preparation for over a decade. In the course of the 1560s the Huguenot churches had emerged as the unifying core of a formidable political alliance.[1] Although still a minority religion, Calvinism had won adherents in every part of France as well as in every social order, including members of the high aristocracy as well as fighting nobles of the countryside. In many towns, and in certain provinces and even entire regions, it often controlled the governmental apparatus, and could therefore establish military strong points. Locally, and sometimes nationally, it could often count on the support of Catholic ' malcontents ', who were sympathetic to the Huguenots on questions of economic and political reform.

There also existed a broad spectrum of ' peaceable Catholics ', reluctant to provoke a civil war, who were allied to the Huguenots on the issue of religious toleration. In the Estates of 1560–1 a majority of the nobles and the Third were probably in favour of some form of toleration. Indeed, as late as 1576–7 – despite heavy pressure from the government and active propaganda by the early Catholic League – the Estates could not be induced to take a serious stand in favor of repression. They would vote for religious uniformity in principle, but not for the subsidies needed to enforce it.

The Huguenot movement had thus become a formidable party, and by this very fact it was led to modify the attitude of passive resistance it had adopted in its early days. The Protestant confession in France was no longer a beleaguered sect of spiritual converts. The religious commitment of many of its new adherents was alloyed by worldly interests which were bound to be reflected in their sense of tactics. Continued insistence upon martyrdom as the sole response to persecution would thus have caused the movement to disintegrate. The religious leadership itself could not have insisted on that principle without aban-

---

[1] Among good accounts of the factional alignments of the civil wars are E. Armstrong, *The French Wars of Religion : Their Political Aspect* (London, 1904) and Romier, *Le Royaume de Catherine de Médicis*.

doning its hope that all of France would soon be brought within the ambit of its teaching. By the early 1560s the Huguenot party was cautiously moving towards a policy of meeting force with force, at least where provocation was extreme. The government, therefore, could no longer impose religious uniformity without protracted civil war.

This barrier to persecution was apparent to informed opinion and also to the government itself. From the standpoint of pure dynastic interest, the obvious strategy was toleration. But in the face of mounting Catholic pressures, that policy could be imposed only by a resolute and energetic king in control of all resources of the state; and in the 1560s the dynastic interest was weak. After the death of Henry II in 1559 the crown was transmitted first to Francis II and then to Charles IX, both of whom were minors at the time of their accession. Throughout the decade, therefore, the government was conducted by a regency which was badly split. The dynastic interest was represented by the queen mother, Catherine de Medici. Although she was inclined at times to toleration, her position was particularly weak since she was not only a woman but a foreigner. The Protestant interest was represented roughly by the Bourbons, or at least a section of that house. The Catholic interest was championed by the House of Guise, which was then the most powerful family of France apart from the ruling dynasty itself.

Governmental policy was thus a makeshift compromise that could not be effectively enforced. Beginning in 1562, the government repeatedly promised a limited degree of toleration. But its toleration edicts were never fully sincere and were often ignored or sabotaged by the judicial establishment. The result was intermittent civil war, with the government normally ranged upon the Catholic side.

In the 1560s the Huguenot response had been moderated ideologically. The Huguenot leadership still had lingering hopes that a peaceful solution could be found. The Counter-Reformation had not yet gathered full momentum, and the government was obviously inclined to some degree of toleration. For many reasons, furthermore, the Huguenots themselves were inclined to hew closely to legality as long as this seemed at all feasible. A modest posture was not only inherent in their moral attitudes; it was also a dictate of good tactics. As a minority party, the Huguenots could not afford to show impatience.

The leaders, therefore, publicly maintained, and perhaps believed at times, that aggression against them by the state was at the instigation of scheming Catholic princes who had imposed their will upon the regent and the king. Resort to arms could then be justified as resistance to a mere usurper. By this and similar pretexts, relations to the regent and the king could be tenuously maintained even in the midst of civil war. The Huguenots could defend their positions, and even go on the offensive, while still avoiding an open challenge to the king's authority. In the 1560s restraint on both sides was so great that informed opinion was often tempted to believe, each time a truce had been concluded, that a peaceful settlement was possible.

But in 1572 a direct confrontation could no longer be avoided. Catherine, caught between two poles, had constantly tended to appease the stronger, Catholic side. This inclination, furthermore, was not only imposed by the balance of domestic forces, but by the strongest diplomatic reasons also, since she was deeply fearful of the prospect of a war with Catholic Spain. But the more she moved in the direction of the Catholics, the greater seemed the menace of the Huguenots. They gradually took on the aspect of a state within a state which balked her authority internally, and which carried on an independent, anti-Spanish foreign policy that was seemingly designed for the ruin of her dynasty. These suspicions were all the easier to hold since Catherine was simply too shallow, intellectually and morally, to appreciate the deeper religious and emotional forces that held the Huguenots together. So far as she could see, the opposition to her policy was the work of a factious, even treasonous conspiracy which 'ought' to disappear and could be removed by force and fraud. In this fashion a weak and incompetent government finally decided on a criminal solution to its difficulties. The St Bartholomew's Day Massacre was designed to accomplish riddance of the Huguenots by assassination of their leaders.

The remnants of the Huguenots were thereby driven to more radical positions. The crime of 1572 could not be blamed on a usurper. It was publicly approved by Charles IX, who by then had come to his majority. Charles was thus the tyrant, and it was against him that the Huguenots took arms. This choice of larger grounds was partly a spontaneous expression of outrage and revulsion, but it was perhaps also a tactical necessity. The movement, badly stricken, might not have responded to less militant appeals.

The doctrine of legitimate resistance had been muted in the Calvinist tradition but was not completely absent. Scholastic concepts of resistance had been taken over by the Reformation, either directly or via republican versions current in Italian and German city-states. There were, of course, important modifications or refinements. Luther and Calvin had been sternly uncompromising in excluding resistance to established authority on the part of private individuals. If the title of a tyrant were otherwise legitimate, resistance by the ordinary subject was a violation of the law of God which forbade resistance to the higher powers. Exception was made for deliverers specially summoned to the task by God. For the ordinary private subject, however, there was no recourse but flight or martyrdom.

But resistance on the part of duly constituted powers underneath the tyrant was another matter. Since the high magistrates beneath the king could also be regarded as established powers who held their sword of God, they might use

43

it to defend His law.[2] Although Luther barely hints at this, and Calvin admits it only guardedly, their reticence was perhaps more tactical than principled. The idea was general in Reformation circles, and it was applied in last resort by Luther's followers as well as Calvin's. In its *Admonition* of 1550, the rights of lesser magistrates were invoked by the Lutheran town of Magdeburg to justify resistance against Charles V.[3] In a work of 1554 much the same idea was mentioned by Calvin's disciple, Theodore Beza (de Bèze) who was to become the spiritual leader of the Huguenots and, later on, the successor to Calvin at Geneva.[4]

This earlier notion of the rights of lesser magistrates was vague and amorphous in its legal grounds. But in the 1570s it was given a firmer foundation in the French tradition of limited monarchy. The resistance theories of Beza and the Huguenots now depended on a radicalized version of the French constitution which was first developed in the *Francogallia* of François Hotman.

The *Francogallia* was an exploration of certain trends already present in the French antiquarian tradition. Although published in 1573, and thus after the St Bartholomew's Day Massacre, it was more than a *livre de circonstance*. The form of the work, and one of its intentions, was a learned reconstruction of French constitutional antiquities, the design for which was probably projected and partially fulfilled in the later 1560s as part of Hotman's general program for a new study of French domestic law.[5] It is difficult to say exactly how radical his early findings were, since the *Francogallia* was finally put together, or perhaps rewritten, at Geneva after Hotman fled from Bourges in order to escape assassination.

Hotman's version of the ancient constitution depended on two new discoveries, or emphases. One was the finding, massively documented from the chroniclers, that the French kingship had been anciently elective. The other was the showing that the public council of the realm, or ancient *Parlamentum*, was coeval with the state itself. That some sort of folk assembly had existed in the early days was also indicated by the chroniclers, and for an even earlier period by Tacitus and Caesar. With Hotman, as with Du Haillan, these early convocations were readily equated with the later Three Estates; and the Three

---

[2] The fullest treatment is Richard R. Benert, ' Inferior Magistrates in Sixteenth-Century Political and Legal Thought ', unpublished doctoral dissertation (University of Minnesota, 1967). For a brief survey, see Julian H. Franklin, *Constitutionalism and Resistance in the Sixteenth Century* (New York, 1969) pp. 19–46.

[3] *Ibid.* p. 31. See also Cynthia G. Shoenberger, ' The Confession of Magdeburg and the Lutheran Doctrine of Resistance ', unpublished doctoral dissertation, Columbia, 1972, especially chs. II and V.

[4] In his *De haereticis a civili magistratu puniendis.* See *ibid.* p. 98.

[5] Ralph E. Giesey, ' Why and When Hotman Wrote the *Francogallia* ', *Bibliothèque d'Humanisme et Renaissance*, XXIX (1967) pp. 583–611. More recently J. H. M. Salmon has been able to date important parts of the work from 1567. See *Times Literary Supplement*, 11 December 1969. A very full study of Hotman's intentions will soon be available in Donald R. Kelley, *Hotman* (forthcoming).

Estates of Hotman's time were taken as a substitution for the people as a whole.

Putting these two main thoughts together, Hotman could contend that the ancient public council was not a creation of the kings, as the other antiquarians had held, but that kings were created by the people meeting in its council. The obligation of the king to remain within the law could then be understood as the condition of his elevation. The institution of election was thus a contract between king and people that was repeated with every new incumbent.

The proof that conditions were imposed, and also the fundamental content of these conditions, was regular supervision by the public council. Consultation by the king was required on every high affair, including not only legislation but the appointment of officials and decisions as to war and peace. The function of the council, furthermore, was not merely to approve or to permit, but seemingly also to decide. Hotman comes very close at times to saying that the public council was the seat of sovereignty.[6]

The institution of election, with which a royal promise was associated, also implied that a king could be rightfully deposed for flagrant violation of his office. Historical evidence in support of this contention was taken from the many instances in which kings of France had been driven from the throne. All of these, for Hotman, had been justified by tyrannical behavior or manifest incompetence and had somehow been sanctioned by the people. They were thus legitimate invocations of a right of deposition.

Despite alterations worked by time, the ancient constitution was supposed to have retained its basic shape. The institution of election had been gradually replaced by the ' Salic ' rule of primogenitive succession. But this, in Hotman's view, was not a change in the duties or status of the office, but only in the method of selecting an incumbent. The kingship was still transmitted by the people's will, which was now expressed in customary public law. At the time of Hugh Capet, furthermore, the offices of dukes and counts, which had been originally filled by election in the council, were given hereditary status. This, for Hotman, was a more serious diminution of the council's power, although he was not quite willing to call it illegitimate. The change, which the council was supposed to have approved, had not affected basic principles. The hereditary magistrates could still be regarded as the people's agents, since they held of the kingdom, not the king.

Most serious of all was the institution of the Parlement at Paris and the transfer to it of many high functions of the council together with its ancient name. Hotman, who as a legal reformer and a Huguenot despised the Parlements, branded their sovereign powers a usurpation, and all but overtly demanded

---

[6] Franklin, *Constitutionalism*, pp. 73, 86. A new variorum edition of the *Francogallia* edited by Ralph E. Giesey and translated by John H. M. Salmon is forthcoming in Cambridge.

restoration of the rights of the Estates. The Parlement of Paris was portrayed as a recent invention by the late Capetians designed to rid them of control by the Estates. It was not a Roman Senate but a ' counterfeit ', and was preferred to the Estates by scheming kings because it was easily corrupted and controlled.

Yet even so, held Hotman, the ancient constitution lived. The Estates had still to be assembled on matters of extraordinary import; and they were still entitled to remove a tyrant. But what if the Estates were prevented by the tyrant from assembling? Hotman's answer is pointedly conveyed by a highly colored version of the War of the Public Good against Louis XI, who was often cited as a tyrant by contemporaries. When Louis temporized in order to escape controls, the nobles took to arms and compelled him to assemble the Estates, which then took measures to reform the government. The implication, therefore, was that the higher magistrates, who held their office of the people, could initiate resistance in its name.

It was this conception of resistance that was now to be generalized and developed by the Huguenot theorists. Among the best known statements, the earliest and most incisive was Beza's *Droit des magistrats*, which was anonymously published early in 1574. Much the same idea is also to be found in the anonymous *Réveille Matin des François* published in that year, and also in Du Plessis-Mornay's *Vindiciae contra tyrannos*, which was probably begun about that time but was published, pseudonymously, only in 1579.

Hotman had already claimed that the right of holding public council was found not only in France but in many other kingdoms. Observing the great benefits derived from this arrangement in so many cases, he had claimed that the right of the council was required by the *jus gentium*, or common law of peoples. Beza now attempted to illustrate this right for every known kingdom considered to be civilized, and could thus conclude that a right so fundamental and so universal was based upon the law of nature. Not only must every legitimate kingship originate by free consent, but no community, in giving its consent, could be presumed to have agreed to absolute authority.[7] The absence of institutional restraints was presumptive proof of illegitimate coercion. It was inconsistent with rational and self-evident conditions of public welfare and the maintenance of justice. In this fashion the French constitution, as Hotman had understood it, was taken as a universal standard to which every other proper kingship was assimilated, and which was universally confirmed by experience and reason. In Beza's list of eminent parallels, special emphasis was laid on the English and Spanish constitutions.

For Beza, and all other reputable Huguenots, initiation of resistance by ordinary subjects was still forbidden absolutely. In this respect the French Calvinists differed from the Scotch and English, who were willing to admit individual resistance at least in last resort. According to Beza, the Estates alone

[7] *Ibid.* p. 107.

had the power to depose, and where the Estates could not assemble, or were hopelessly corrupt, the initiation of resistance belonged to the magistrates alone. But this was simply intended to prevent the ' excesses ' of democracy and to protect the Huguenots from the charge of general subversion of the social order. It was not understood as a serious bar to resistance in the existing circumstances. Beza generally assumed that the magistrates, confronted with a tyrant, would act in their corporate capacity. But he also implied that where the magistrates collectively have failed to do their duty, a single magistrate may sound the call to arms, especially if he occupies a major office of the kingdom as a whole. In the *Vindiciae contra tyrannos* these implications were explicitly endorsed.[8] Hence despite the ban on initiative by private subjects, a legitimate procedure could be found in almost any circumstance.

The general trend, indeed, was toward a constant radicalization of this aspect of the doctrine. The *Vindiciae contra tyrannos* was more permissive than the *Droit des magistrats*, and the writers of the later Catholic League, who built on Huguenot conceptions, were more permissive than their adversaries. Holding the majority position, they were less in need of giving reassurances.

On the substantive issues of this period, Bodin's position was generally liberal.[9] In the dedicatory letter to the *Methodus*, the reformist program of the Chancellor L'Hôpital is echoed in the call for the codification of French law, and Bodin's sympathy for other aspects of that program is broadly indicated in his discussion of the French regime. In the *République*, points of public policy are taken up at length, and in these chapters Bodin takes note of almost all the grievances, and embraces almost all the remedies, that were put forward in the *cahiers* of this period and that were taken up in reforming royal ordinances. Among other things, he attacks the sale of offices, the use of mercenary troops, and the custom of expensive gifts to favorites. Above all, he proposes that the burden of taxation, which he saw as a fundamental threat to political stability, should be gradually reduced through repurchase and improved administration of the crown's domain. In economic policy he was even in advance of contemporary thought in finding the key to French prosperity in natural and human resources rather than in precious metals.[10]

On the highly sensitive question of religious policy, Bodin was also liberal. Outwardly at least he was a Catholic. But his private religious meditations, which he dared not publish in his lifetime,[11] were an unusually daring as

---

[8] *Ibid.* p. 194.

[9] For a brief sketch of Bodin's overall position, see Julian H. Franklin, ' Jean Bodin ', *International Encyclopedia of the Social Sciences* (1968) 2, pp. 110–13.

[10] For the text of Bodin's tract on economic theory and commentary on it, see Henri Hauser, *La vie chère au XVIe siècle, La response de Jean Bodin à M. de Malestroit* (1568) (Paris, 1932). See *République*, vi, 2, for various references to this polemic against bullionism.

[11] The manuscript of the *Colloquium heptaplomeres de rerum sublimium arcanis abditis*

well as idiosyncratic development of the humanist tendency to deemphasize dogmatic conflicts. In the course of his restless effort to harmonize religious differences, he gradually came to that sense of their underlying unity which, in the sixteenth century, was the starting point for theories of toleration. The true, or natural, religion, in which Bodin believed, was his own combination of Jewish monotheism with neo-Platonizing speculation.[12] The different positive religions could then be understood as variations on this universal truth in the realm of sense impressions. They could not be refuted as mere errors since the evidence that each invoked on its behalf ultimately depended upon faith. Nor could they be branded as pernicious. Sincere worship in any of the positive religions, as distinct from mere superstitions, was acceptable to God. There was therefore no intrinsic reason to persecute religious dissenters as perverse or insincere. At the end of the *Colloquium heptaplomeres*, the seven interlocutors, representing the major religions, agree to disagree in friendly recognition of their differences.[13]

Bodin, however, was too impressed by the political advantages of religious uniformity to make religious freedom a fundamental right. On the practical level his recommendations were strictly ' politique '. Where religious uniformity existed, it ought to be maintained by law. To permit religious innovations would encourage the development of factions in the state. Where, on the other hand, a new religion was already present, and could no longer be removed by force except by endangering the state, toleration was the wiser course. In this situation the goal of religious uniformity was best promoted by a calculated blend of coercion and example. The king could show his disapproval of the new religion by keeping its adherents from positions of eminence and power. The mass of dissidents might then be persuaded to return, since it was the natural tendency of subjects to follow the example of their princes.[14] Outright persecution, on the other hand, would only confirm them in their opposition.[15]

Bodin's recommendations were thus substantially in line with the qualified and provisional toleration habitually proffered by the government in the truces of the civil war. It was not a generous policy, but in the circumstances of the

(1593?) was burned at Bodin's request upon his death, but unauthorized copies circulated in manuscript form. No printed version appeared until the nineteenth century, and no complete version until 1857.

12 On Bodin's religious thought in general, see Pierre Mesnard, ' La pensée religieuse de Bodin ', *Revue du seizième siècle*, xvi, 1929, pp. 71–121, and also Georg Roellenblek, *Offenbarung, Natur, und jüdische Überlieferung bei Jean Bodin* (Kassel, 1964), and also, ' Der Schluss des *Heptaplomeres* und die Begründung der Toleranz bei Bodin ', paper delivered at *Internationale Bodin Tagung* (Munich, 1970). The importance of Bodin's notorious belief in demons for his religious evolution is reappraised by C. R. Baxter, ' Jean Bodin's Daemon and his Conversion to Judaism ', paper delivered at *Internationale Bodin Tagung* (Munich, 1970).

13 *Colloquium heptaplomeres de rerum sublimium arcanis abditis*, L. Noack, ed. (Schwerin, 1857) p. 358.

14 *République*, iii, 7, pp. 496–8 (380–2). 15 *Ibid*. iv, 7, p. 564 (537).

time it was probably the most that one could reasonably expect. Bodin, more-over, was sincere in his commitment. At the Estates of Blois he would be a stalwart opponent of religious war against the Huguenots.[16]

Bodin, then, was not too distant from the Huguenots on immediate political objectives, and this parallelism in his attitudes also extended to his moral evaluation of the royal court. To a large extent he accepted the Huguenot explanation of the St Bartholomew's Day Massacre, although he does not mention the event explicitly.

This appears from the preface to the *République*, which is grave and sombre in its tone. Confident as late as 1572, Bodin had been encouraged to believe that civil warfare had been permanently settled by the wise decree of a benevolent king whose words had been accepted in good faith by the more sober part of the community.[17] Now confidence had disappeared, and the ' shipwreck ' of the state could be envisaged. Two great errors that promote distrust are men-tioned, one of which is the current doctrine of legitimate resistance. But the other, and the one discussed at greater length, is the mistake of those who ' instruct princes in the rules of injustice to insure their strength by tyranny, than which there could be no basis more ruinous to power '.[18] Machiavelli is the source of this mistake and is represented as the evil genius by whom such counsellors are guided. This portrayal is a striking change in Bodin's esti-mate. Machiavelli had been saluted in the *Methodus* as the first of the moderns to revive the ' civil science ' of the ancients.[19] Now he is singled out as the arch atheist and destroyer of commonwealths.[20]

Bodin does not say explicitly that these counsels had been adopted under Charles IX. But he is obviously alluding to a familiar contention of the Hugue-nots. On their account, Machiavelli was the ultimate architect of the St Bartho-lomew's Day Massacre. His poisonous teachings had been brought to France by Catherine de Medici along with her Italian counsellors. The crime of 1572 was thus the work, not only of a tyrant but of foreigners.[21]

---

16 See below, pp. 90–1. Reformist and tolerationist motives could have played a role in Bodin's apparent involvement in the *Politique* conspiracy of 1574, although he could have been drawn into the plot simply as a result of his personal connections to the Duke of Alençon in whose service he was then engaged. The conspiracy, formed in anticipation of the death of Charles IX, was to bypass the rightful successor, Henry, Duke of Anjou (who was then also king of Poland) in favor of his more ' liberal ' younger brother, Francis, Duke of Alençon. On Bodin's apparent role, see A. Garosci, *Jean Bodin : politica e diritto nel Rinascimento francese* (Milan, 1934) p. 33, and especially Kenneth D. McRae, ' The Political Thought of Jean Bodin ' (unpublished doctoral dissertation, Harvard, 1953) pp. 57ff.

17 *Methodus*, p. 211 (259). (This reference introduced only with edition of 1572.)

18 *République*, preface.

19 *Methodus*, p. 167 (153).

20 *République*, preface.

21 See Donald R. Kelley, ' Murd'rous Machiavel in France: A Post Mortem ', *Political Science Quarterly*, LXXXV, no. 4, December 1970, pp. 545–59. The best known Huguenot polemic is Innocent Gentillet, *Anti-Machiavel* (Geneva, 1576).

Bodin's shift to absolutism is thus surprising at first thought. Cautiously liberal on public policy and alarmed by the trend of royal tactics, he might have been expected to maintain a middle course and to lay even greater stress on institutional restraints. That he failed to do so is even more surprising in view of his earlier stance. Why did he now abandon a constitutional position that he had so firmly supported but a few years earlier? [22]

Bodin himself supplies no explanation because he saw no need to do so. In the *République* sovereign power is simply defined as absolute without any explanation of the grounds or any indication that a change in his position had occurred. For Bodin, apparently, the new definition of supremacy was but a clarification of what he had previously maintained, and he seems to have come to it intuitively. We can, however, make certain inferences as to the kinds of intellectual operations encompassed in that intuition.

The shift to absolutism was evidently occasioned by Bodin's profound unwillingness to acknowledge legitimate resistance. To deny the right of resistance with respect to a particular authority is to consider that authority as absolute. It can be argued that no legal obligation can be absolute. But that is to raise a different question. At the very least, Bodin was justified in thinking that if an authority was less than absolute, a right of resistance could not be denied.

In 1566 he had not examined the relation between resistance and limited supremacy. In one passage, he had suggested in passing that the right of deposition is incompatible with sovereignty. The existence of that right in Germany was one reason, very briefly mentioned, why the German Emperor was not a proper monarch. But for kingships like the French, which he believed were limited yet sovereign, the issue of ultimate obligation was evaded. In the manner characteristic of the antiquarians, he had used the language of prediction. He simply observed, approvingly, that tyrants have been frequently deposed.[23] The legal right of deposition had been therefore left ambiguous.

But in the 1570s the issue of resistance was presented as a working ideology that seemed to have dramatic consequences. Reflecting on the causes of the civil war, Bodin concluded that the mere belief of a community that it was entitled to resist a tyrant was inherently pernicious. We have indicated that in

---

[22] In 1572 Bodin undertook his one and only revision of the *Methodus* without introducing any substantial alteration of its constitutional perspective. There is even some evidence that he remained committed to his earlier view as late as 1573. After the election of Henry, Duke of Anjou (later Henry III of France), as king of Poland, Bodin was a member of the French delegation that welcomed the Polish ambassadors at Metz. Bodin may have written, or at least helped to compose, the address of Charles des Cars, which was strongly constitutionalist in tone. For a careful review of the evidence, see McRae, ' Political Thought ', p. 59, and also Moreau-Reibel, *Jean Bodin*, pp. 214–15, 273–4. We might also note that the tone of the *Politique* conspiracy of 1574, in which Bodin was implicated, was vaguely constitutionalist (see Georges Weill, *Les théories sur le pouvoir royal en France pendant les guerres de religion* [Paris, 1891] pp. 136ff) although Bodin's personal interest in this movement is unclear. [23] *Methodus*, p. 192 (217).

the preface to the *République* he fixed on two great errors fatal to a common-wealth, one of which is addiction of the ruler to the arts of tyranny. The other is the mistake of those who propagate the doctrine of resistance:

But there are still others, directly hostile to these [counsellors of tyranny], who are no less dangerous and are maybe even more so. These are the ones who under the pretext of exemption from burdens and the people's liberty cause subjects to rebel against their natural princes, and thereby open the way to licentious anarchy, which is worse than the severest tyranny that ever was.[24]

The text of the *République* is even more explicit. To admit that resistance is legitimate is to encourage the subjects to rebel:

Many, indeed, would be the tyrants if it were allowable to kill them! The king who laid too many taxes would be a tyrant. The king who ordered anything the people didn't like would be a tyrant, on Aristotle's definition in the *Politics*. The king who kept guards for the safety of his life would be a tyrant. The king who punished conspirators against his state with death would be a tyrant. How could good princes be certain of their lives?[25]

Had the point been left at this, it would have been a simple judgment on political psychology. But Bodin took a further step. He intuitively concluded that the right of resistance in a people was inconsistent with sovereignty as such. If he had been able to articulate his argument, his reasoning might have gone like this:

A limited authority may be resisted;
A supreme authority acknowledges no superior or equal;
An authority which may be judged and deposed by its subjects acknowledges a superior;
Therefore, a limited authority cannot be supreme;
Supreme authority is absolute.

On this construction of his underlying thought, Bodin was simply extend-ing his earlier judgment on the status of the German Emperor to every prince whose authority was limited. Since a true sovereign was irremovable, a prince was either absolute or he was not a sovereign at all. Although the argument is never stated in this order, the underlying logic is sometimes suggested in reverse. Particularly revealing is the following passage from the *République* on what kind of prince may be resisted:

[We] have to know whether the prince is absolutely sovereign (*absoluement sou-verain*), or whether he is not a sovereign. For if he is not absolutely sovereign, it follows necessarily that the sovereignty must be in the people or else the nobles. In this case, there is no doubt that it is licit to proceed against the tyrant.[26]

The questionable element in Bodin's intuition is the third premise of the argument as reconstructed, which asserts that the people is above a king if it has the power to depose him. A political authority that acknowledges a right

[24] *République*, preface.   [25] *Ibid.* II, 5, p. 307 (225).   [26] *Ibid.* II, 5, p. 301 (221).

of deposition in its subjects does not, by that alone, acknowledge a superior within the law. The right of deposition is not necessarily a power pursuant to law, in the sense of a judicial verdict. In the case of a limited monarchy, it is simply a declaration that the ruler has abandoned the rights and protections of his office by deliberate and flagrant transgression of the conditions of obedience. The right of resistance thus comes into play not by means of established procedures but in order to preserve them. Thus construed, it is consistent with supremacy, although not with absolute supremacy.

Yet Bodin's error is understandable enough. The logic of limited supremacy required considerable ingenuity. It was not developed until late in the seventeenth century, and even then it seemed to be extremely odd.[27] Writing in a less sophisticated period, Bodin could hardly have been expected to see it, and given his political preferences he had no reason to invent it. There is, indeed, no evidence that he was ever aware of any problem. It is not as though his earlier idea of sovereignty had been a reasoned concept which he then deliberately abandoned. His notion of limited supremacy had merely been implicit in his usage, and the issue of ultimate obligation had been left ambiguous.

It is important to point out, moreover, that the later equation of supreme with absolute was neither foolish nor utterly unworkable. The term ' supreme ' is sometimes used that way in ordinary discourse; and the concept can be adapted to limited monarchies and other constitutionalist systems by admitting division of supremacy. This perhaps is not the most illuminating way of looking at it. But it was the path adopted by many writers of the seventeenth century.[28]

Hence the main difficulty in Bodin's later theory is not so much the absolute definition of supremacy as the principle of indivisibility. Although the latter principle was wrong on almost any definition of supremacy, the new definition of supremacy made it less adaptable to France. Bodin, however, showed not the slightest inclination to rethink the principle, or even to revise its application. All the authorities that he had deemed sovereign in 1566 were still assumed to be so.

Yet, on the whole, the new conception of supremacy was added to his old identifications of the sovereign with surprisingly little embarrassment. His empirical demonstrations of the unity of governmental functions were not affected by the change, and his locations of the legislative power in city-states reputed mixed, and also in the German Empire, were no more wrong (or right) on the new conception than the old. The main problem in his former treatment of city-state arrangements was his failure to see the implication of a veto in certain forms of senatorial ' advice '. In the *République* he simply continued to ignore it.

The French constitution, and others like it, thus presented the most difficult problem, since Bodin had already organized the evidence to support a case for

[27] Samuel Pufendorf, *Law of Nature*, VII, 6, 10, pp. 1070ff.   [28] See below, note 29.

limitation. But there were certain factors, best called psychological, that helped to sustain him in a new interpretation.

We have already noted that no reputable commentator of the 1560s had seriously contended that the French constitution was a mixture. Bodin himself had never entertained this possibility, and saw no reason to entertain it now. He continued to believe that the king of France 'alone' was sovereign and that every writer worth considering agreed on this. The only question now was to define more precisely what was meant by sovereignty. From this perspective, he need not have thought that his new version of the French constitution was a serious departure from what he had previously held. Persuaded now that absolute authority was an analytic implication of supremacy, he could have felt that he was simply removing an element of ambiguity which had become apparent on a deeper view of sovereignty.

By the 1570s, to be sure, the Huguenot theorists were beginning to develop a concept of divided sovereignty that was reasonably adequate to the constitution of a limited monarchy.[29] But Bodin would never see this point. Although many portions of the *République* were an implicit answer to the Huguenots, he paid surprisingly little attention to the specifics of their doctrine.[30] So far as he could see, the Huguenots were simply contending that sovereignty lay in the Estates, and many of their statements, at least in the early 1570s, could have easily been read that way.[31]

Hence, for all Bodin could see, there was nothing in the French tradition that clearly indicated an intermediate solution between popular sovereignty and absolutism. Given his new way of looking at the concept of supreme authority, and given also the element of ambiguity surrounding many of the legal precedents, his path towards an absolutist interpretation of the French constitution could not easily be halted by the evidence.

[29] On the distinction between the 'real' sovereignty of the people and the 'personal' sovereignty held of the people on condition by the prince, see especially Beza, *Right of Magistrates* in Franklin, *Constitutionalism and Resistance*, pp. 110–13, 128–9. For the subsequent history of this influential distinction, see Otto von Gierke, *Natural Law and the Theory of Society*, Ernest Barker trans. (Cambridge, 1934; reprinted Boston, 1957) pp. 54ff, and also John H. M. Salmon, *The French Religious Wars in English Political Thought* (Oxford, 1959) pp. 52ff.

[30] There is only one specific reference to any Huguenot writing. In *République*, 1, 8, p. 137 (95) he speaks of those who have written on the 'devoir des magistrats', which is probably a reference to Beza's anonymously published *Droit des magistrats*. The characterization is finished in a phrase, and nowhere in the *République* is the specific doctrine examined. The *Francogallia*, on the other hand, is discussed without being named only at the end of the *République* in a chapter dealing with the advantages of successive over elective kingship. Bodin seems reasonably clear on Hotman's position as to original election, but neither here nor elsewhere does he indicate direct familiarity with other aspects of the work. He may have known of it only at second hand through the refutations of Antoine Matharel. On Bodin's relation to the Huguenots, see John H. M. Salmon, ' Bodin and the Monarchomachs ', paper delivered at the *Internationale Bodin Tagung* (Munich, 1970).

[31] On the movement of the Huguenot doctrine from quasi-republicanism to limited monarchy, see below, p. 103.

CHAPTER 4

The Case for Absolutism

Bodin's case for royal absolutism is not presented as a systematic demonstration in which the supporting evidence is massed together, and opposed interpretations stated and rebutted. The counter-arguments are touched on here and there, but almost always in peripheral settings. In Book I, chapter 8, which deals with the meaning of sovereignty, the absolute status of the king of France is simply assumed, and embarrassing evidence explained away. This procedure is not inherently illicit. It is a way of showing that all apparent limitations on the king of France, and on other rulers that Bodin believed were sovereign, were actually compatible with absolutism. But the initial assumption of absolute authority, around which the evidence is organized, is laid down so dogmatically that the actual import of the evidence is all too frequently discounted by fallacies of reasoning and gross distortions.

The two main arguments against absolutism, which Bodin sought to overcome, had both seemed decisive earlier. One was the rendering of oaths of coronation, or other solemn promises, on the part of rulers whom he now considered absolute. The other was the regular practice, common to the kings of Europe, of consulting the Estates or Parlements. For a modern student, this second fact would seem to be the more decisive for the locus of constitutional authority since it bears directly on the legislative process. In Bodin's mind, however, the coronation promises posed an even deeper question, and it is these that he considered first.

His essential strategy in construing sovereign promises is to show that they do not involve a perfect obligation to maintain existing law. This is not because an absolute authority cannot become liable to a binding obligation. Bodin, like most other writers of the time, very strenuously insists that a properly contracted obligation is sanctioned by the law of nature, as well as civil law, and is as fully binding on a sovereign as it is on private individuals.[1] His reason for believing that oaths of coronation may be compatible with absolute authority is the element of flexibility that seemed inherent in the promises, not their intrinsic nullity.

The oaths most difficult to handle were those in which the wording was specific – in which, that is, the ruler explicitly and specifically promised that he would maintain existing law. To Bodin's knowledge the king of England

---

[1] *République*, I, 8, pp. 152ff (106ff). See below, p. 80.

was the only contemporary sovereign whose oath was unmistakably specific.[2] But he was also willing to admit, on the authority of Pedro Belluga, that the kings of Spain (or Aragon) often made specific promises subsequent to coronation. According to Belluga, who was now Bodin's main authority on Spanish matters, many of the *fueros*, or common usages of Aragon, were literally ' contracted laws ' (*leges pactionatae*), which the kings had promised to maintain in exchange for grants of subsidies.[3] Moreover, the kings of France, Bodin admits, had also given promises to keep the law.[4] These, unlike the Spanish, seemed merely isolated cases. Yet even so, the existence of specific promises by sovereigns was too common for the issue to be by-passed, and Bodin's answer on this point is extremely revealing of his basic argument.

His solution, very simply, is that the promise of a king, like the promise of any individual, ceases to be binding by the law of nature once the reasons for keeping it have ceased to operate. In the case of royal promises to maintain specific laws, the reason for maintaining them is the interest of the community in the utility or justice of the laws. If this utility and justice cease with a change in circumstances, the king's obligation ceases also. A valid promise to maintain the law is thus compatible with absolute authority. As long as the community retains an interest, the promise is completely binding. But the king can always change the law on his finding that this interest has lapsed.[5]

Although this solution was prompted by the Spanish contract laws, which were less comprehensive and perhaps less solemn than an oath of coronation (at least as Bodin understood them) there was nothing in the principle to prevent its extension to both kinds of oath. ' Henry VII [of England] ', he notes, ' was always seen to make use of his sovereign power, even though the kings of England are not consecrated except in swearing that they will keep the ordinances and customs of the land. For this [English] oath should be related to what we have said above '.[6]

The last phrase refers to his general comment on the Spanish promises and, more specifically, to a statement on the oath of ancient Epirus which applies the principle, derived for Spain, to oaths of coronation :

[2] He should have included the king of Spain as well, since the oath of Aragon was also specific. Bodin refused to credit a very restrictive and menacing version of that oath which Hotman and Beza had publicized in France. He was right not to do so since the Huguenot version was inaccurate. But he came to this conclusion mainly on inferential grounds, some of which were highly dubious, and he made no serious efforts to determine the exact phraseology of the oath that was actually taken. Since he did not believe that the mere presence of specific language was constitutionally decisive, his neglect is not surprising. For his discussion of the Huguenot version of the Spanish oath, see *ibid*. p. 130 (90). For a full treatment of the sources of the Huguenot version, see Ralph E. Giesey, *If Not, Not : The Oath of the Aragonese and the Legendary Laws of Sobrarbe* (Princeton, 1968) chs. VI, VII, and especially pp. 238ff.

[3] Pedro Belluga, *Speculum principum ac justitiae* (written 1438–41) (Paris, 1530) p. 4.

[4] *République*, I, 8, p. 146 (p. 101).

[5] *Ibid*. p. 134 (93).

[6] *Ibid*. p. 139 (96).

And if someone should say that the kings of the ancient Epirotes swore that they would rule well and duly according to the laws of the land, and that the subjects also reciprocally promised that they would maintain and keep their king according to the laws of the land: I say, that, notwithstanding all these oaths, a sovereign prince can change the laws, or annul and quash them, once they have ceased to be just.[7]

Bodin's position is thus a very simple argument from the flexibility of promises. But this simplicity is easily hidden from the modern reader by a number of tangential observations and irrelevant citations included in his general reflections. Before passing judgment on the principle itself, it seems well to comment on these observations in order to forestall mistaken inferences.

At the point of taking up the Spanish promises Bodin declares that a contract and a law are very different things and must not be confused. The point is repeated several times as though it were of great importance. Belluga, among others whom he does not name, is taxed for having failed to recognize it. It is as though Bodin were suggesting, in explanation of the Spanish promises, that an act of legislation can never be the object of a contract.

But this seems not to be intended. As far as I can see, the sole purpose of the distinction is to show that an act of legislation is not *per se* a contract. French legislation of the period normally included clauses of solemnization which declared the law to be perpetual, and Bodin was anxious to point out that this was not to be taken as the indication of a binding promise. The essence of the legislative act, he argues, is the component of command, or expression of the ruler's will. But a ruler cannot be subject to his own command solely by virtue of some intention not to change his mind. That would have to be a promise to himself, and according to the Roman legal maxim, no obligation can arise solely from a promise to one's self.[8] Bodin, accordingly, is not denying that an act of legislation can be the object or consideration of a promise or a contract. He is simply contending that it is not *per se* a contract.

Why he should have felt that previous writers had confused this point is more difficult to understand, and is probably to be explained by hasty reading of the texts. The Italian civilians had regularly held that a royal contract is like a law in that the courts must treat it as a public regulation; and they had also held that under certain circumstances an act of legislation must be treated as a contract. In a standard illustration, the statute of a city, which offered citizen rights to immigrants in the hope of attracting newcomers, would become a binding contract with respect to any person who had come to settle in consideration of the city's offer.[9] This idea occurs in passages that Bodin cites

---

[7] *Ibid*. p. 135 (93–4).   [8] *Ibid*. p. 132 (91–2).

[9] Jason de Maino, *Consilia sive responsa* (1516) (Venice, 1581) I, *cons*. I, 15, fos 3r–3v. A passage cited *inter alia* in Bodin's marginalia is a comment by Baldus on *Code*, 5, 16, 6, part of which goes as follows: ' A contract concluded with the Emperor or Empress has the force of law . . . Hence note that a contract sometimes passes into law, and, vice versa, that a law

disapprovingly. But it has little to do with the thought that laws *per se* are contracts. Above all there is no indication in Belluga of any confusion between laws and contracts in his account of *leges pactionatae*. A *lex pactionata* is the object or consideration of a contract, but is not *per se* a contract.

One other possible target of Bodin's criticism is the opinion of certain humanist civilians that the Roman Emperor had been bound by his own legislation with respect to his conduct in personal relationships.[10] The principle here is that one who gives a rule to others is bound by it himself. This is not to say that the act of legislation is a promise, nor does it deny the power of the Emperor to change the rule by a further act of legislation. Bodin, however, may well have thought it did.[11]

In another deceptive observation, he contends that a king is entitled to full restitution (*restitutio in integrum*) if he enters any contract that seriously impairs his sovereignty.[12] The analogy in private civil law was the petition for restitution in full where a disadvantageous contract had been entered into by a minor, or as a result of unreasonable fear, or deliberate fraud, or had done serious damage to the maker beyond half the value of the consideration. The use of this as an analogy for royal promises involving sovereignty is dubious and would be sharply criticized by Grotius.[13] Nevertheless, the analogy is not intended by Bodin for the question posed by contract laws and oaths of coronation. It seems clear from context that he is thinking of international treaties involving large cessions of domain or of sovereign prerogatives. Whatever his objections to the validity of contracts of this sort, he does not apply them in his construction of the Spanish promises. The standard objection to the cession of domain by treaty was the alienation by the ruler of powers belonging not to him but to the commonwealth.[14] No such difficulty was involved in agreements between the ruler and the corporate community of which he was the chief.

A final pitfall for the reader is the contention that the engagement of the Spanish king is to be regarded not as a contract, but a promise – that it is best

sometimes passes into an express or implicit contract. . . . Hence resident aliens (*comitatenses*) who have been received into a municipality [as citizens] at some given time by law, cannot be put back into their former status. Therefore, if anything contained in the 'aw as a formal gift has passed over into an implied contract, the act is thus irrevocable. For no even the Emperor can revoke a contract made with him unless for cause, as when the consideration owed to him is not fulfilled.' The same example was also offered in Bartolus' comment on *Digest*, i, 1, 9, *Commentarii*, i, f. iir.

10 Thus, for example, a celebrated comment by Jacques Cujas on the meaning of *legibus solutus*. See *Observationes et emendationes*, xv, 30 in *Opera* (Prato, 1836), i, cols. 703–4.

11 In spirit, at least, the humanists' attempt to narrow the meaning of *legibus solutus* expressed their general discomfort with absolute authority. Cujas' reasoning thus appears in Beza in support of the more general contention that the prince was subject to existing law in his legislative capacity as well. See Franklin, *Constitutionalism and Resistance*, p. 127.

12 *République*, i, 8, pp. 133–4 (92).

13 *On the Law of War and Peace* (1625), F. W. Kelsey trans. (Oxford, 1925) p. 381.

14 See below, pp. 76ff.

regarded as an engagement entered into from love of justice and the public weal and not in consideration of a gift of subsidies.[15] It might thus appear that Bodin is preparing to relax the obligation on the king by holding that a promise is less binding than a contract. But this again would be mistaken. His only purpose, in denying the occurrence of a contract, is a courtly bow to the virtue and nobility of kings. Since a deliberate promise is as binding as a contract for Bodin, he sees no reason to derive the obligation of the Spanish king from sordid motives of mercenary gain.[16] Even then, he makes no effort to maintain his little fiction, and a few passages later refers to the promises as contracts. The two forms of obligation are thus considered equivalent and Bodin uses either term without distinguishing their legal implications.

With these extraneous reflections clarified, it becomes fully clear that Bodin's position on specific promises rests on nothing more than the simple proposition that we noted earlier. A promise to maintain existing law ceases to be binding on the king if the law becomes unjust.

Very narrowly defined, this conclusion would seem justified. In contracts between private parties, or in ordinary contracts between the public and a private person, the legitimate ground of non-performance, where the contract was valid to begin with, would be non-performance by the other party. In Bodin's present application, the cause of non-performance is extended. It is now related to the fact that the purpose of a promise to maintain a set of laws is the interest of the community in the usefulness or justice of the laws. But ' the cause ceasing, so also the effect '. If the laws become incompatible with justice and the public welfare, the community, to which the promise has been given, can have no reasonable basis to insist upon performance.

It is at this point that difficulties seem to enter. Bodin seems right in holding that a contract ceases to oblige if neither party has an interest in seeing it performed. But this is not to say that the set of facts which end the obligation may be unilaterally determined by the king. If the promise was valid to begin with, it conferred a right on the community, which is as much entitled as the king to judge the conditions of performance. In private law, cessation of an obligation would depend on mutual consent unless the maker of the promise were forgiven by the courts. But where the parties to the promise are the king and the community, the ultimate authority is the law of nature, not the courts.[17] Forgiveness of the promise would thus require the consent of the community, unless, of course, it is to come to civil war. It follows, therefore, that an absolute king, who makes a valid promise to maintain existing law, is no longer an absolute authority, and can no longer act without the consent of the com-

---

15 *République*, 1, 8, p. 134 (93). 16 *Ibid.* p. 134 (93).

17 The same might apply to a contract between the public and a private subject if the courts were not accorded the position of a final arbiter. But this kind of engagement would hardly involve a promise to maintain existing law, and would not be constitutionally significant. For Bodin's position on contracts between the sovereign and a private individual, see below, pp. 8off.

munity. To say that he continues to be absolute is to deny that a valid promise has occurred.

Bodin, however, repeatedly asserts that the king alone may determine the justice of a law that he has sworn to keep. He does remark, offhandedly, that repeal of such a law would require a specific *non-obstante* clause.[18] But he treats this as a mere formality designed to show the courts that repeal is deliberately intended. In principle, at least, there is no significant distinction between the status of a law that has been promised and an ordinary act of legislation. Both are subject to repeal on the unilateral finding of the sovereign that alteration of the law is to the interest of justice and the public welfare.

Bodin's solution to specific promises thus depends upon a contradiction, and one so obvious and blatant as to cause him serious embarrassment:

Thus a law and a contract must not be confused. Law depends on him who holds the sovereignty, since he has the ability to obligate all his subjects but no capacity to obligate himself. On the other hand, a convention between the prince and his subjects is mutual. It obligates the two parties reciprocally, and neither of the parties can contravene it to the prejudice of the other and without the other's consent. In this case the prince is in no better position than a subject, except, as we have said, that when a law that he has sworn to keep ceases to be just, he is no longer bound by his promise. This is something that subjects cannot do among themselves unless they are relieved of [obligation] by the prince.[19]

Bodin's only justification of this odd result is drawn from practical necessity. He repeatedly, and properly, observes that the statutory law of any commonwealth must be changed from time to time with changing circumstances. From this he concludes that a sovereign authority cannot be strictly bound by an oath to maintain existing law. Were it otherwise the legislative power would be crippled and change could not be introduced. The sovereign who takes an oath must therefore be permitted to retract it, even though he may be perjured in the sight of God.[20]

Applied to democratic states, this reasoning has some persuasiveness, and it is, indeed, to ancient city-state democracies that Bodin mainly turns for his illustrations of the principle. He could readily point to a number of instances in which the people of city-state republics had sworn to keep a statute or a set of statutes, and had been forced by sheer necessity to go back upon their oath.[21]

Bodin, however, would extend this reasoning to monarchies as well as aristocracies, and this generalization does not work. The promise of a prince, unlike the promise of a whole community, does not fetter the legislative power, but merely alters the conditions of its exercise. The law could still be changed, but there would have to be consent from the community. Hence the sole effect of

---

[18] *Ibid.* p. 134 (93).
[20] On the question of perjury, see note 24 below.
[19] *Ibid.* p. 135 (93).
[21] *République*, 1, 8, pp. 147–9 (102–3).

a royal promise to maintain the law is to create, or to confirm, a situation of limited supremacy.[22]

It is the failure to recognize this outcome that is the ultimate weakness in Bodin's account of specific royal promises. At the time of the *Methodus*, he had explicitly accepted this result. But now that he had come to an absolute definition of supremacy, the earlier solution necessarily appeared as some species of divided sovereignty, and this he had never understood. For one brief moment he entertains the possibility. But he dogmatically and almost violently rejects it as a threat to his most cherished doctrine:

But it has to be one way or the other. The prince who swears to keep the civil laws is either not a sovereign, or else he is perjured if he contravenes his oath; and it is inevitable that the sovereign prince will contravene it in order to annul, change, or correct the laws according to the exigencies of situations, times, and persons. Or if we say that the prince continues to be sovereign and yet is bound to take the advice

[22] On two occasions Bodin cites a group of passages from Baldus, Nicholas Tudeschis (Panormitanus), and Alessandro Tartagni (Alexander Imolensis) as authority for his view on sovereign promises. All had held that a statute sanctioned by an oath (*statutum juratum*) could be repealed like any other statute, if sufficient cause existed. This opinion was fairly widespread in the civilian-canonist tradition. According to Baldus, who supplied an influential rationale, the ordinary rule is that a sworn statute may not be repealed, that repeal in violation of the oath is perjury, and that perjurers do not have power. But he then puts forward an important qualification: ' This is to be understood unless a just cause supervenes, because in any oath the clause " if things remain the same " (*clausula rebus sic se habentibus*) would seem to be inherent . . . For if novelty emerges, a novel remedy is needed.' Comment on *Code*, 6, 42, 19 in *Praelectiones*, IV, f. 147r.

I doubt that opinions of this sort bear on royal promises, which is the controversial issue in Bodin. Almost all the jurists I have looked at seem to be thinking of the ' statuta ' of city-states when they comment on the *statutum juratum*, rather than the *leges* or ' constitutiones ' of the Emperor or prince. One exception is Alessandro Tartagni, who asks, in one of his *consilia*, whether the oath of a Pope is strictly binding if he swears that he will not appoint a Cardinal unless the incumbent Cardinals approve his choice. Responding negatively, Tartagni applies Baldus on the *statutum juratum* to a monarchical system, and he uses general language which must have made a deep impression on Bodin. ' A superior ', Tartagni says, ' who makes a statute even with an oath against repeal affixed may repeal that statute for cause with impunity, his oath notwithstanding '. Yet despite this language, the grounds of the actual holding are narrowly circumscribed. In answering objections, Tartagni observes that if the Pope, whom he believed was absolute, were strictly bound by an oath requiring him to have consent, it would change the constitution of the Church. But this could not be admitted, since the constitution of the Church is established by the law of God. It thus appears that the central part of Tartagni's case is grounded theologically. *Consilium*, VI, 224 in *Consilia*, 3 vols (Venice, 1597) II, fos 150v–1r.

Given the complexity of these opinions, and the ambiguities of their language, Bodin's use of them is understandable. But in view of the French tradition on royal promises, and his own view in the *Methodus*, we cannot assume that Bodin was simply swept along by the suggestiveness of language in the sources. He was led to his idea of royal promises from abstract reflections on the meaning of supremacy. For other opinions on royal promises in the French writers of the sixteenth century, see Chasseneuz in the passage quoted above, p. 13; and Hotman, *Consilium* 131, *Operum primus (-tertius) tomus*, 3 vols (Geneva, 1599–1600), II, cols 606–14. For a commentator who repeats the standard view on *statuta jurata*, yet explicity insists that royal promises to keep the law or to refrain from certain acts are binding, see Pufendorf, *Law of Nature*, I, 6, 4, p. 92; VIII, 10, 3, p. 1343; and VII, 6, 10, pp. 1068ff.

of the Senate or the people, we must also say that he may be dispensed by the subjects of the oath he took to keep the laws inviolate. And the subjects, collectively and individually, who are bound and obligated to the laws, will also have to receive dispensation from their prince, or else be culpable of perjury. Thus will sovereignty be sundered in two parts, and now the people, now the prince, will be the master – which is an egregious absurdity and utterly incompatible with absolute sovereignty as well as contrary to the laws and natural reason.[23]

The basic line of reasoning may thus be put as follows. Since supreme authority is absolute and indivisible, a promise to maintain existing law on the part of a prince who continues to be sovereign is absurd and contradictory. There are, however, certain states in which such promises are given and which have to be considered monarchies. For such exceptional cases we are bound to assume that the sovereign's promise may be retracted unilaterally on his determination of good cause. But if the promise was attended by an oath, the prince may be culpable of perjury.[24]

This, then, is Bodin's way of accounting for awkward coronation oaths. But given the odd results and his views on the question of perjury, it is with an obvious sense of relief that he turns to the French coronation oath, which seemed to him to be free of specific phraseology. ' The oath of our kings ', he says, ' which is the fairest and most succinct there is, carries no implication of maintaining the laws and customs of their predecessors.'[25] The French oath is thus interpreted as a simple promise to act justly, which would not be constitu-

---

[23] *République*, i, 8, p. 148 (100–1). It might also be worth pointing out that the change from absolute to limited monarchy brought about by a specific promise would not be an illegal alienation of sovereignty. The rule of inalienability is designed to protect the community, which is here the willing beneficiary.

[24] This view on perjury seems to have been suggested by Tudeschis' comment on *Decretals*, iii, 5, 25, in *Super Tertio Decretalium* (Lyon, 1559) fos 34v–5r. Baldus and Tartagni seem not to hold that repeal of a *statutum juratum* is necessarily accompanied by perjury. In holding that every oath contains a *clausula rebus sic se habentibus*, Baldus would seem to be providing an escape. Tudeschis seems to hold an opposing view on perjury, and the rationale, which he does not supply, is probably to be found in a passage from Bartolus which Bodin almost surely knew, even though he does not cite it in this context. In holding that *statuta jurata* may be altered, Bartolus considers the objection that an oath, which is taken subject to retraction, would be devoid of consequence and purpose. ' But this is not persuasive ', he replies, ' because no one can impose a law upon himself from which he may not depart . . . And the oath will have sufficient consequence, because by virtue of the fear that it inspires, the step of revocation will not be taken lightly.' A distinction is thus drawn between the legal and the religious obligation. A *statutum juratum*, says Bartolus, ' can be repealed, although those who revoke it are perjured '. Comment on *l. omnes populi* (*Dig.* i, i, 9) in *Commentarii*, i, f. 13v. (For a jurist of the early sixteenth century who takes over this opinion, see Ulrich Zasius, also on *Dig.* i, i, 9, in *Opera omnia*, Lyon edition of 1550 reprinted by Scientia Verlag [Aalen, Germany] 7 vols, 1964, i, col. 263.) This other view was more attractive to Bodin, in part perhaps because he was a man of deep religious feeling, and in part also because he wished to warn rulers not to take such oaths or, if they did, to honor them as far as possible. He must have recognized that the abrogation of promises could be a serious danger to the king himself. Too often used, the right of repeal would undermine good faith between the king and the public.

[25] *République*, i, 8, pp. 135–6 (94).

tionally significant. In the absence of specific indications as to how the promise must be carried out, the obligation would be fully compatible with absolute authority in Bodin's understanding of that term. The king would still be free to alter law as he saw fit, and to act according to his conscience without the consent of any other party. Even should he violate his conscience by flagrant transgression of the law of God or nature, there would be no right conferred upon his subjects to offer forcible resistance. On Bodin's interpretation, forcible resistance to an absolute authority is generally forbidden by the law of God. Accordingly, a general promise to act justly on the part of a king who was absolute in Bodin's sense would imply no more and no less obligation than would exist in the absence of that promise. In either case the king would be subject to the law of God and nature, but would be accountable to God alone.[26]

On certain assumptions, this conclusion seems to be correct. General language issued voluntarily on the part of an absolute authority could well be taken as a pious expression of benevolent sentiments. In the absence of a clear commitment to perform, there would be no binding promise, and no right conferred on the community. But this is not necessarily the case. If the promise were exacted from the king by the community as a condition of continuing obedience, and if the community's object in imposing that condition were to subject its sovereign to law, the promise would be binding despite the absence of specific language.

In 1566 the French coronation oath had been so regarded by Bodin himself. He had then believed that the kings of Europe had been forced to take such oaths in confirmation of long-standing efforts of their subjects to insure the rule of law. The promise of the king was thus considered to be binding and specific. In the *République*, however, an identical version of the oath is reinterpreted as general solely on the basis of the language, and without regard to the circumstances of its origins or the traditional opinion of the commentators. Even so, it may be noted, the case for generality is dubious, since in some of the phrases there are terms that sound suspiciously specific. A good example is the reference to ' due law ' in the phrase *debitam legem atque justitiam . . . conservabo*.

This failure to consider the historical circumstances in the case of overt oaths helps explain Bodin's complete inattention to implicit promises. Although these are not discussed at all, they cannot be excluded *a priori*. If an act of legislation is clearly less than a command; if it is evidently conceded by the prince to assure the good will of the community, it would appear to create an obligation. Obvious cases of constructive promise, articulated in the French tradition, include laws expressly promulgated at the request of the Estates, and customs long in use that the kings have explicitly or even tacitly confirmed.

[26] *Ibid*. p. 128 (88–9).

The first part of Bodin's argument thus depends on outright contradiction or on *a priori* dismissal of the evidence. In the second portion of his argument the existence of absolute authority is proven more directly from the characteristics of the legislative process. He seeks to demonstrate that the validity of royal acts, in France and other European kingships, does not depend upon consent. The main problem was to show that the various routines of consultation exhibited in all these systems were essentially advisory and optional. Here again the solution is extremely strained. It implicitly assumes that all departures from the consultative routine are conclusive proofs of absolutism – that the exceptions to the rule, in other words, are definitive indications of the legal norm.

Thus Bodin does not deny that the French Estates were frequently consulted before a law was passed. He even tends to excessive generosity in calling this procedure usual. But the frequency of consultation does not seem juridically significant. The decisive point for him is the existence of a number of cases in which important rules of law were altered unilaterally:

And not to go to other countries, we in this kingdom have often seen certain general customs repealed by edicts of our kings without hearing the views of the Estates, when the injustice of the existing rule was obvious (*oculaire*). Thus the custom of this kingdom applying to the entire region of the customary law (*pays coustumier*), concerning the right of inheritance by mothers and the status of their children's property, was changed without assembling either the general or regional Estates. Nor is there anything new in this, since from the time of Philip the Fair, the general custom of the entire kingdom, which did not allow a plaintiff who had lost his case to be charged with the payment of the court expenses, was annulled by edict without assembling the Estates. And the general custom which prohibited the receipt of testimony from women in civil cases was abolished by edict of Charles VI without convening the Estates. For it is necessary that the sovereign prince should have the laws within his power so that he may change and correct them according to the situation.[27]

In Bodin's way of looking at the problem, these exceptions are dramatic proofs of absolute authority and thus reveal the purely optional status of the usual procedure:

But as to general and local customs . . . it has been the practice not to change them without a right and proper convocation of the three Estates of France in general, or of each of several bailiwicks, even though the king is not required to follow their advice, and can do the opposite of what they ask, if natural reason and the justice of his will should prompt him.[28]

In arriving at this judgment, Bodin is obviously correct in noting the existence of exceptions; and he is also justified in refusing to admit that common practice is juridically decisive in and of itself. The frequent repetition of

[27] *Ibid.* p. 142 (98). [28] *Ibid.* p. 137 (95).

a practice does not necessarily imply that the community conceives it to be 'right', and would take all deviations as wrong. But at the same time the existence of a legal norm is not necessarily disproven by pointing to exceptions. Many of the cases mentioned by Bodin could be squared with the usual procedure by assuming tacit authorization. As he himself suggests, in many of the situations where the ruler acted unilaterally the injustice of the rule was 'oculaire'. For other cases that he might have mentioned, a distinction could be drawn between rules of secondary interest, on which unilateral action was permissible, and more important rules, on which some indication of consent was necessary. Still other cases might be dismissed as simple illegalities, and denied the force of precedent. Although this last solution requires much sophistication, it was not beyond Bodin. In dealing with the Roman constitution, he is aware of many 'successful' – in the sense of unpunished – deviations from what he takes to be the legal norms. One example has to do with harsh punishment of Roman soldiers by the Senate, in violation of the usual procedure because it was done within the city limits and in the face of tribunitian intercession. 'To make short answer', says Bodin, 'I cite the maxim of Papinian that one must not argue from what was done at Rome but rather from what ought to have been done'.[29]

The existence of a legal norm is thus revealed by what is generally accepted as correct. In the absence of all other indications, the usual procedure by itself would be persuasive evidence that consultation was required for some purposes. Where this procedure was associated with a widely held belief that the king was subject to the law, and where the requirement of consultation was often mentioned or suggested by the legal commentators, its normative status is even more strongly recommended. But in Bodin's argument these additional considerations are excluded or ignored.

The basic weakness in his method is even more dramatically revealed by his treatment of the English precedents in which the tradition of consent was less uncertain. Bodin himself observes that the English Parliament was extremely bold in its behavior toward the king, a characteristic which he attributes to the Northern temperament.[30] He also believes, on the authority of Polydore Vergil, that the English Parliament had always been assembled at regular intervals.[31] But this and other evidence is utterly discounted on the mere relation of the English ambassador that Henry VIII had no hesitation in acting unilaterally. The legality of this, or even its legal rationale and frequency, are not considered to be interesting questions. The mere fact of some exceptions by some ruler seems to be dispositive:

It might still be said that ordinances made by the king of England at the request of the Estates cannot be annulled without convoking them. That is the usual practice, and it is ordinarily done this way, as I have learned from the English ambassador, Mr Dale, who is a man of integrity and learning. But he has assured me that

[29] *Ibid.* p. 232 (168). [30] *Ibid.* p. 139 (96). [31] *Ibid.* p. 140 (97).

the king accepts or refuses laws [i.e. petitions from the Parliament] as he sees fit, and that he does not abstain from commanding laws at his pleasure and against the will of the Estates, just as Henry VIII was always seen to make use of his sovereign authority.[32]

But there were certain cases, noted by Bodin, in which the authority of the Estates or Parlements seemed to be explicitly acknowledged. Laws were sometimes passed not only at the request of the Estates, or subsequent to consultation, but with their formal ratification or endorsement. The most familiar example for Bodin was the examination and approval of legislation by the Parlements, which might be considered for this purpose as the authoritative voice of the community. He was not aware that analogous endorsement was the usual procedure in the English Parliament. But he did acknowledge that this device was occasionally employed.

He did not believe, however, that there were any circumstances in which the use of this procedure was obligatory. The purpose and effect of ratification, as he saw it, was to foreclose potential opposition. The act of endorsement by the court or the Estates was a formal waiver of objections which was binding not only on the ratifying body but on all subordinate authorities. From the standpoint of the king, the device was a matter of convenience which he was free to omit at his discretion:

And as to the verification of edicts, done by the Estates or by the Parlement, it is of great consequence for making sure that they are kept (*pour les faire garder*), which is not to say that the sovereign prince could not make law without it.[33]

This solution is precarious in two respects. As Bodin himself suggests, the king, in seeking ratification, responds to objections in advance. Concessions are made to the ratifying body in exchange for its cooperation. Depending on the circumstances, the offer of concessions could be construed as an implicit promise by the king to maintain the law as promulgated until such time as he is released by the ratifying body. Bodin, who pays no attention to implicit promises, ignores this possibility.

The other, and perhaps more fundamental, question is the anticipated opposition which the ratification is intended to forestall. If the opposition could be constitutionally legitimate, it would be a sign that the king is less than absolute. Bodin is ambiguous on this. He seems sometimes to be thinking of mere remonstrations by the magistrate or of extra-legal refusals to enforce. But he also suggests that a law of doubtful justice, which was imposed by a direct command, need not be acknowledged by the courts beyond the lifetime of the king who made it. In comment on an English precedent, it is the foreclosure of this latter possibility which most prominently figures in his explanation of the effects of ratification. Noting that the marriage contract between Mary Tudor and Philip of Spain was finally

[32] *Ibid*. p. 139 (96).   [33] *Ibid*. p. 149 (103).

ratified in Parliament 'after many disputes and difficulties', he goes on to describe the legal consequences:

I have chosen to quote this verification at length to show that the entire sovereignty belongs undivided to the kings of England, and that the Estates are only witnesses (*n'y ont que voir*). For verification by the Estates, no more than verification by a court, a Parlement, a corporation, or a guild, does not suffice to show power to command. It is rather consent to validate enactments (*consentement pour valider les actes*) so that doubt may not be cast on them after the queen is dead, or even while she lives, through opposition from the magistrates and officers of the kingdom.[34]

I am not sure that even this account is ultimately consistent. It is hard to see how the command of an absolute prince, which was initially valid by his sole command, could later be deprived of force through the act of any agent other than the king himself or his successor. But this difficulty is not immediately obvious, and the possibility of subsequent disallowance of commands (although usually not by magistrates) is one that Bodin frequently invokes.[35]

The issue of disallowance naturally leads us to Bodin's position on the powers of the courts, which will conclude our presentation of his arguments. In any political system the overt behavior of the higher courts in admitting or refusing orders, together with the judges' own estimation of their powers, is particularly persuasive evidence as to the state of constitutional norms. In French practice, the sovereign courts had consistently maintained that they would enforce no order in conflict with existing law unless it was recommended to them by strong considerations of justice or the public welfare. The form of their contention, which was generally accepted by the legal commentators, was the right to suspend promulgation of an order until such time as their objections had been satisfied.

In the *République*, these contentions of the courts are almost totally ignored. The senatorial claim to powers of review by the Parlement of Paris, which was a very old and basic component of the French constitutionalist tradition, is all but summarily dismissed. Bodin is willing to admit that the Parlement had once been the Senate of the realm and still held that title honorifically. But he believes that it had lost the legislative functions of a senate at the time when it was turned into a standing court. In any event, the true functions of a senate are not juridically significant since it follows, from all the principles of good administration, that the proper duty of a senate is simply to provide advice.

The sole evidence for these contentions, apart from general reflections on the best organization of a state, is a group of royal edicts that attempted to restrict the right of remonstration with respect to legislation. Even on Bodin's

[34] *Ibid.* p. 141 (98).　　　　　　　　　　　　　　　[35] See below, pp. 73–4.

account the edicts were a recent effort to alter an established practice, and the court, which had bitterly protested their legality, had refused to abide by them in practice:

And yet as far as remonstrations by the court are concerned, because of the difficulties it caused in publishing the letters patent issued at Rouen on the 16th of August, 1563, the king said to a delegation from the court: ' I do not wish you to meddle in any other business but the provision of good and speedy justice. The kings my predecessors put you where you are for that alone, and not to make you my tutors, or the keepers of my town of Paris. And when I give you a command, and you find any difficulty, it will always be agreeable to me that you should present your remonstrations. And after they are made, I wish to be obeyed and have no more retorts.' Nevertheless, the Parlement raised still other remonstrations since there was a *partage* [stipulated division of opinion] on the publication of the aforementioned letters. This gave rise to a decree of the Privy Council on the 23rd day of the September following which declared the *partage* null and forbade the Parlement to take deliberation on ordinances emanating from the king which concerned affairs of state. This had already been done by letters patent issued in 1528.[36]

The right of protracted remonstration is considered once again in connection with the judicial duties of the magistrate. At this point the absolute power of the king is simply presupposed. Bodin proceeds as if all the evidence needed to establish its existence had already been adduced in his reflections on the force of royal promises and on the relation of the king to the Estates. He finds no occasion, therefore, to consider the behavior and opinion of the courts as an independent issue. The basic position of the judge is simply derived by logical deduction from the principle of absolute supremacy. An initial right to remonstrate is conceded and is clearly recognized.[37] But the right to persist in remonstrations is definitively excluded as incompatible with the sovereign status of the king.[38] Where the remonstration has been overruled, and the ruler's will is shown to be inflexible, the magistrate is bound to yield. The one, very cautious, exception to this rule is an order so unmistakably and gravely in conflict with the law of God or nature that it would be clearly sinful for the magistrate to execute it.[39] Yet even so, his resistance must be passive.

Bodin's case is therefore very thin. But its persuasive force is not to be gathered solely from the evidence adduced. It is sustained at every point by a deep-seated fallacy of reasoning which powerfully affected Bodin's judgment of the facts. The influence of this fallacy is especially noticeable in his treatment of the role of the Estates. Throughout his discussion of consent, he is at pains to show that they have no power to command. The Estates, he observes, do not assemble or dissolve upon their own initiative but only at the king's command. When they are assembled, their requests for legislation are not

---

[36] *République*, III, 1, p. 358 (266–7).　　　　[37] *Ibid.* III, 4, p. 423 (320).
[38] *Ibid.* p. 426 (323).　　　　[39] *Ibid.* pp. 413–4 (312).

addressed in the language of demand, but in the form of humble supplications which the king is free to grant or refuse as he sees fit. It is thus established that the Estates do not have *imperium*, or ' power '.[40]

This account is more or less correct for France and is not too implausible for England.[41] The serious problem is that Bodin concludes, from the absence of power to command, that consent is not required either. The reader may have noted this *non-sequitur* in some of the passages already quoted. It is also particularly manifest in the following comment on the form of procedure used in the Estates:

And what semblance of popular power can there be in the assembly of the Three Estates, seeing that each person individually and all collectively bend their knees before the prince and address humble requests and supplications which the king accepts or rejects as he sees fit.[42]

The missing link in this *non-sequitur* is Bodin's theory of sovereignty. A political authority is either supreme or is completely subject. Since the Estates, as their procedures indicate, make no pretension of supremacy, and even acknowledge the king's superiority, they must surely be completely subject.

The impact of the fallacy is even more extensive; in one form or another, it colors the entire argument. Bodin ' knew ', beyond all doubt, that the king of France was sovereign. He had always thought so, and so also had everybody else. He also knew, from his further reflections on supreme authority, that sovereignty was absolute as well as indivisible. It therefore followed inescapably that the king of France was absolute, and it also followed inescapably that the facts must somehow fit. The entire case is thus colored by a *petitio principii*:

> Sovereign authority is absolute;
> The king of France is sovereign;
> The king of France is absolute.

The minor premise of this syllogism is simply taken over from Bodin's findings of 1566. But when it is joined together with his revised definition of supremacy, it is really a conclusion which he ought to prove.

But the persuasive power of the fallacy from Bodin's point of view seems even more impressive when it is restated in the form of a *non-sequitur*. According to the later theory of sovereignty, the prince of an independent commonwealth must either be absolute or else subject to the command of the Senate or Estates. In the latter case he would not be a king at all, but the prince of a polyarchic system like the Emperor of Germany or king of Poland.

---

40 *Ibid*. 1, 8, pp. 138–9 (95–6).
41 In a passing reference to Aragon, apparently to the Cortes of 1265, Bodin hurriedly passes over the promise to maintain the privileges of the Estates by James I. *Ibid*. p. 139 (96). Bodin contends that the promise was not binding on successors. On this problem of the continuity of contracts, see below, pp. 8off.　　　　42 *Ibid*. II, 1, p. 263 (192).

But the king of France was obviously not subjected to the command of the Senate or Estates, and he was not in the position of the German Emperor or king of Poland, on which account he must be absolute.[43]

Yet this is not to say that Bodin was utterly naive, or that his underlying fallacy was easy of detection for contemporaries. The elements of ambiguity contained within the French tradition permitted his case to be connected to it without the appearance of an overt breach. The obligation of the king to keep existing law had always been presented tactfully. It had been considered binding for all foreseeable occasions, but the invocation of absolute authority had not been totally excluded. The role of the Estates had not been specified precisely in the older commentators; and there was even some uncertainty attaching to the status of the Parlements. The right of protracted remonstration was virtually a right of veto, yet not exactly that. The courts, moreover, had occasionally been forced to yield. They had attempted to maintain their right in principle by the notation *de expresso mandato* and had often reasserted it successfully. But although they had remained unbroken, they were not unbowed.

In Bodin's presentation, these elements of ambiguity were systematically resolved in favor of the king. The general bearing of the precedents was no doubt distorted in the process. But for a Frenchman of the time, it might have been difficult to say exactly where this distortion had occurred. To one who was royalist in sympathies, it could have appeared that Bodin was simply being more precise on what sovereignty ' had ' to mean. This, indeed, was Bodin's own conception of his enterprise.[44]

But there was yet another element that lent his argument appeal. In the construction of his case for absolutism he was extremely respectful of the validity of fundamental law. In one way or another he managed to incorporate at least some of the legal limitations that had been traditionally considered indispensable. Although this accommodation was sometimes purchased at the cost of inconsistency, Bodin was obviously sincere. In order, therefore, to estimate his aims precisely and to understand the meaning of his doctrine, this other side of his absolutism must be taken up in some detail.

[43] The fallacy comes very close to the surface at *ibid.* 1, 8, p. 135 (93) where he takes up the force of specific coronation promises. The promise of the German Emperor is binding, that of the king of the ancient Epirotes is not. The implicit rationale, very clearly suggested by the context, is that the former is subject to the Estates and the latter is not subject.

[44] Book 1, ch. 8, which is the key theoretical chapter on sovereignty, purports to be nothing more than the precise definition of a term used by all people under different names, but one which ' no jurisconsult or political philosopher has defined '. *Ibid.* p. 122 (84).

CHAPTER 5

Limitations on Absolute Authority

The limitations acknowledged by Bodin were divided into two broad classes. Some were derivations from the law of nature and looked mainly to the protection of the rights of individuals. The others were positive fundamental laws which guaranteed the continuity and resources of the crown itself, and which Bodin refers to as *loix royales* or *leges imperii*. Since the theoretical issues posed by the latter are more complicated, it seems better to begin with them.

In the French tradition, the idea of fundamental law, if not the term itself, often included every form of constitutional restriction – procedural as well as substantive, positive as well as natural. Bodin's usage, consistent with his absolutism, is inevitably more specialized and narrow.[1] Only two fundamental laws are mentioned, both of which may be technically regarded as mere creations of a right in the successor. The law of succession to the throne, which is one fundamental law, is the rule that determines the successor. The law against alienation of the royal domain, which is the other fundamental law, establishes a right in the successor to undiminished use of all the resources of the office. Bodin correctly thought that both these rules were not only basic for political stability but were also fully compatible with absolutism.

It is with respect to the law of succession that the theoretical relationships are clearest. In any stable order there has to be a rule of continuity which is ultimately the same as the law that identifies the rightful sovereign. In republics, where the sovereign person is collective, the test of continuity, and indeed of legitimacy, is the rule of selection and form of procedure that identifies the ruling corporation. In monarchical states the same function is performed by the law of succession to the throne. It is the test by which a legitimate incumbent can be distinguished from a mere usurper.

Depending on the specific form of the monarchy, this rule may be a more or less severe restriction on the freedom of incumbents to name their own successors. In purely patrimonial kingships, the incumbent may be technically free to bestow the crown on whom he pleases, although he is obviously bound to some degree by the rule of consanguinity. In France, on the other hand, all rights of testamentary disposition were technically denied to the incumbent, since the crown descended automatically by primogeniture in the male line.

---

[1] There is a sharp distinction introduced between these two fundamental laws and other well-established rules of common law, which is not encountered in Seyssel and the antiquarians.

With respect to naming a successor, the king of France was as fully limited as the king of an elective monarchy.

Yet even a restrictive rule is compatible with absolute authority. Absolute supremacy does not necessarily imply a right in its possessor to determine situations that arise when he has left the scene. He must, of course, have full juridical authority to determine situations in the present. But this is not affected by denial of his right to name an heir. In other words, the situation that the law of succession seeks to regulate is created by the ruler's death.

This consistency can also be looked at in another way. One test of absolute authority is its immunity from legitimate resistance. But the law of succession to the throne need not give rise, legitimately, to a preventive act of the community directed against the actual incumbent. If an incumbent should designate an heir who is other than the one prescribed by law, his designation is technically a nullity. A pretender, who might later attempt to succeed upon the will of that incumbent, could be rightfully opposed by the community, since he would be a mere usurper. But there could be no occasion for preventive action against the incumbent who made the designation. The sole mechanism for enforcement of the law of succession is the assertion of a claim by the successor that it designates.

In Bodin's formulation, the ideas that we have just set forth are introduced through a succinct but effective distinction between the powers of the royal office and the title of an incumbent to possession of that office. The royal office may be absolute and the incumbent to that office may make use of all its powers for the present. But where the law of succession is restrictive, the incumbent's title to these powers is but a life-possession, or a life-estate. The law of succession to the throne may thus be regarded as a kind of entail annexed to the crown in favour of some designated heir:

And as to laws, like the Salic law, that concern the state of the kingdom and its establishment; – since these are annexed and united to the crown, the prince cannot detract from them. And should he do so, his successor can also annul anything that has been done in prejudice of the royal laws on which the sovereign majesty is established and supported.[2]

No explanation is advanced as to how this annexation came about. But it follows from all that we have said that no special explanation is required. Once an order of succession has been fixed by custom, and in so far as it is firmly fixed, it is beyond the reach of each incumbent and beyond the reach of royal power generally. The Salic law would thus be a special custom of the realm, which differs from most other customs in that a king is impotent to alter it without the consent of the community.

Bodin therefore felt no need to discuss the derivation of the rule, except to show that it was not an outgrowth of original election. According to the

2 *République*, 1, 8, p. 137 (95).

Huguenots, as we have seen, the Salic law was an alteration, introduced by custom, of an earlier and original system of election, the traces of which could still be found in various aspects of the royal coronation. Strictly speaking, this derivation was not incompatible with absolutism. As Bodin himself had said, an elective kingship could be absolute. Nevertheless, the thesis of original election was so closely associated with a constitutionalist version of the history of France that Bodin attempted to oppose it at all costs. He had always thought that the Frankish monarchy in France had been instituted by a conquest,[3] and, faced with the challenge of the Huguenots, he clung to this idea with even more tenacity. Despite the evidence amassed by Hotman, he attempted to refute original election.[4]

Consistent with this view, moreover, Bodin is vigilantly on guard against any version of the coronation ceremony that might be taken as a vestige of original election.[5] According to an old tradition, the kings of France did not acquire full title to their office until they had been formally inaugurated. On this account, as Bodin notes, an interregnum would occur between the death of one incumbent and the installation of the next, in which the business of the state would have to be conducted in the people's name. Since such arrangements seemed too reminiscent of elective systems, he dismisses the tradition as erroneous, and is one of the first important commentators to endorse the maxim that the king never dies.[6] The transfer of power is thus supposed to be accomplished instantaneously without intervention by the public.

A related position that Bodin also scornfully attacked was the assimilation of the Salic law to the *lex regia* of imperial Rome. Certain French civilians of the sixteenth century, including some whose attitudes inclined toward absolutism, had found it convenient to assume that the kings of France received their powers from the Salic law in the same manner that the Roman emperors acquired theirs from the *lex regia*.[7] This might be taken to imply that in France, as in elective systems, the powers of a king reverted to the people on his death and were then conferred upon a new incumbent. In an anecdote,

---

[3] *Methodus*, p. 207 (252), p. 192 (215).
[4] *République*, vi, 5, pp. 983ff (729ff). Bodin's attempted refutation seems to depend on that of Antoine Matharel [with Jean Papire Masson], *Ad F. Hotomani Franco-galliam responsio* (1575).
[5] On the coronation ritual itself, see *ibid*. pp. 984–5 (pp. 730–2). For the opposing interpretation, constantly suggested by the Huguenots, see the *Vindiciae contra tyrannos*, in Franklin, *Constitutionalism and Resistance*, pp. 142ff.
[6] *République*, i, 8, p. 160 (112); iii, 2, p. 386 (288); vi, 5, p. 986 (732). On Bodin's legal formula, see Ralph E. Giesey, *The Royal Coronation Ceremony in Renaissance France* (Geneva, 1960) p. 177. In actual practice, immediate exercise of power by the new incumbent had become the custom in the thirteenth century. But the idea of a kind of interregnum still lingered on, and is used in the *Vindiciae* (Franklin, p. 183) as an indication of original election.
[7] Thus Jean Ferrault, *Tractatus . . . iura seu privilegia aliqua regni Franciae continens* (1515), priv. no. 12, p. 344 (bound together with Grassaille, and continuously paginated beginning at page 319). The king alone, according to Ferrault, is entitled to enact a law ' because by an ancient royal law (*antiqua lege regia*), which is named the Salic law, every right and all power were transferred to the king '.

approvingly recounted by Bodin, the use of the *lex regia* as an analogue for France is rebuked as a subversive utterance.[8]

There were certain situations, to be sure, in which intervention by the public could hardly be denied. Bodin apparently admits that, where a regency was needed, it ought to be approved by the Estates.[9] But this authorization was not an indication of a deeper or more fundamental right. In principle, at least, a regency was conducted in behalf of the incumbent who acquired title by successive right.[10] A more interesting question was posed by the extinction of a dynasty. If the last survivor failed to name an heir, the power passed to the Estates.[11] But this contingency apparently seemed so remote, and so refractory to legal treatment, that it is noted without special comment.

The second fundamental law was the inalienability of royal domain, which embraced the entire complex of valuable rights attaching to the royal treasury – such as public lands and forests; feudal dues and other rents; fees, fines, tolls, and confiscations; and all manner of established taxes. The inalienability of this domain had always been regarded as a fundamental rule of fiscal probity. The domain was supposed to have been set aside in order to provide a king with a source of annual income normally sufficient to defray the costs of government.[12] If the capital were squandered and the revenues reduced, the public was unnecessarily exposed to an increased burden of taxation. Alienation of domain, except in situations of emergency, was thus considered inherently unjust.

The rule of inalienability could also be regarded as a protection of the dynasty itself. If the usual sources of revenue were lost by the sales or gifts of an incumbent, his successors in the kingship would be forced to desperate and dangerous expedients, among which the most ruinous was new taxation since it so often led to revolution.[13] To alienate domain, accordingly, was directly to prejudice the interest and right of the successor. It was to sell or give away the very substance of his legacy.

From either standpoint, however, the rule of inalienability was consistent with absolute authority. Like the law of succession to the throne, the rule was prospective in its force with respect to a particular incumbent. Even on a strictly absolutist version of the rule, a king was not prevented from entire use of the domain as long as he remained in office, and, as long as he remained king, he could leave possession of the domain in the hands of anyone he wished. The only thing he could not do was to transfer a right to the domain

---

[8] *République*, VI, 5, pp. 986–7 (733).   [9] *Ibid.* I, 8, p. 136 (95).

[10] But the right of the Estates to ratify a regency had often been invoked as an indication of ultimate authority. See, for example, the speech of Philip Pot at the Estates of Tours, reported in R. W. and A. J. Carlyle, *A History of Medieval Political Theory in the West*, 6 vols (Edinburgh and London, 1909–36) VI, pp. 176–7 and notes.

[11] *République*, VI, 5, p. 988 (734).

[12] *Ibid.* VI, 2, pp. 856–7 (650–1).   [13] *Ibid.* pp. 860–2 (653–4).

that would endure beyond his lifetime and bind his successors in the kingship. This limitation was no doubt severe, since it warned potential buyers of domain that their title would be insecure. Yet this defect of right in the incumbent was not, technically speaking, a limitation on absolute authority. It simply followed from his temporary possession of that absolute authority.

As with the law of succession, furthermore, a violation of the law of the domain was simply a legal nullity and could not justify preventive action on the part of the community. The mechanism of enforcement was the imprescriptible title of successors to assert their right of use.[14] The law of the domain, finally, could also be easily accounted for. It too was a special custom of the realm that was beyond the reach of particular incumbents.[15]

In the civilian-canonist tradition, all of these relationships are contained in the idea of the domain as a usufruct in public property, or even as a simple right of use, or as something analogous to the right of a husband to a dowry; and these comparisons are taken over by Bodin.[16] In all of these relationships of private law, the user of the property is unable to alienate the title, but in the case of usufruct at least the right of the ultimate owner to enforce this limitation is restricted to subsequent recovery. An illegal alienation, in other words, does not terminate the usufruct, so that the analogy carried over into public law implies no right of preventive action on the part of the community.[17] In

---

[14] *Ibid.* p. 857 (651).   [15] See Lemaire, *Lois fondamentales*, pp. 112–14.

[16] *République*, VI, 2, pp. 859–60 (652–3). Since these ideas were commonplaces no specific derivation need be sought, although it might be noted that Bodin refers readers to Choppin's *De domanio Franciae libri III*, which had appeared in 1574. Choppin's treatise is rich in comparative materials on which Bodin may well have drawn. We may also note that Bodin also mentions, as applicable to France, the Roman distinction between the *fiscus* of the Emperor, which was private property, and the *aerarium* of the state, which was public. This point is made by many commentators of the time in order to emphasize the public status of the domain and to claim for it the same protections accorded the *aerarium* in classical Roman law. However, there was no real parallel in France to the *fiscus*, since the patrimony of the dynasty was public domain.

[17] This implication of the analogy goes unmentioned in the medieval commentators, or at least in the ones that I have checked. It seems simply to have been assumed, and Bodin, repeating the tradition on this topic, saw no need to make the point explicit. But Barclay, writing slightly later, and dealing with the extreme situation where a sovereign alienated the entire kingdom to a foreigner, was to take a position that then moved Grotius to elaborate the point by way of answer. Barclay had said that where the entire kingdom was alienated, not only was the act illegal, but the king who sought to alienate was thereby deprived of his title to the kingdom. Grotius, more cautious, holds that the act is simply a nullity, and then goes on to argue that ' this is the view of the jurists in regard to a usufructuary, to whose position, we have said, that such a king is analogous; by alienating his right to a third person the usufructuary effects nothing. And the statement that the usufruct reverts to the owner of the property must be construed in accordance with the period fixed by law.' *Law of War and Peace*, I, 4, 10, p. 157.

The last sentence of this passage refers to an apparent antinomy in Roman private law between *Institutes*, 2, 4, 3 and *Digest*, 23, 3, 66. According to the first, a usufruct does not revert to the ultimate owner of the property in the event of an attempted alienation by the fructuary; but the second passage could be read to hold the opposite since it says, in effect, that despite the attempted alienation, the usufruct reverts to the ultimate owner.

private law the attempted alienation is simply a legal nullity which cannot debar the true proprietor or the designated successor to the usufruct from full enjoyment of the property at the time the usufruct expires. In public law this situation would occur only at the death of an incumbent king.

There were, inevitably, some exceptions to the rule of inalienability. Under French law there were two situations in which alienation was legitimate. One was the constitution of appanages, subject to conditions of reversion, for younger brothers of the reigning king. The other was sale of the domain, with provisions for repurchase, in order to raise money for a war emergency.[18] According to Bodin, and most other writers of the time, alienation in this second situation required the consent of the Estates.[19] Yet even this was compatible with absolutism. Consent was simply regarded as one of several conditions which, if properly met, would foreclose any claim by a successor. But if this or any other condition were ignored, the successor would be entitled to recover.

On the other hand, there were some provisions of French law for which this remedy did not suffice. According to the Edict of Moulins of 1566, donations of domain for a limited period of time, or the farming of taxes at rates below the market value, were to be considered alienations of domain, and the courts were enjoined to disallow them.[20] Since the purpose of such rules was to prevent donations on a temporary basis – to prevent, as it were, the transfer of the fruits of the domain as well as transfers of the title – the abuse that they attempted to prevent could not be compensated by subsequent recovery of use.[21] To this extent, Bodin's conception of inalienability was a weakening of the French tradition. Although he clearly disapproved alienation of the fruits, he did not specify this prohibition as a principle of fundamental law and could not have done so without endangering his absolutist principle.[22]

> Grotius, ingeniously and also persuasively, I think, reads the second passage as if it said that, despite the alienation of the usufruct, the act is of no effect, and the usufruct will revert to the ultimate owner at the expiration of its term just as it would have, had no attempt at alienation occurred.

[18] Edict of Moulins, par. 1 in Isambert, *Recueil*, 14, p. 186. Hence in principle at least the rule of the sixteenth century is more restrictive than that suggested by the medieval commentators. The latter permitted alienations if the damage to the successor was not severe. See Bartolus on *Digest*, 43, 23, 3, *Commentarii*, v, f. 148v.　[19] *République*, vi, 2, p. 859 (652).

[20] Edict of Moulins, par. 5 in Isambert, *Recueil*, 14, p. 187.

[21] Unless perhaps by suit against the occupant for the value of his use, which would not, of course, be a sure remedy. The Edict of Moulins, it may be noted, frequently speaks of prevention by the courts, although this, from a purely royalist standpoint, would be a right conferred by statute and one that the king could override by a derogatory clause.

[22] But the idea of a duty in the king to conserve the fruits of the domain for public purposes was so traditional, that at one point he casually includes it: ' And so sovereign princes are not permitted to abuse the fruits and revenues of the domain, even if the commonwealth is at peace and completely free of debt, for they are not its fructuaries but its users (*usagers*, Lat. *usarii*) only, and once they have taken what they need for their household and the commonwealth, they must save the surplus for [future] public necessity.' *République*, vi, 2, p. 860 (653). See also I, 9, p. 182 (130).

The basic conception of these fundamental laws was also extended to the inalienability of sovereignty itself as distinguished from valuable domain. On this very complicated topic Bodin's remarks are curiously brief and fragmentary. But since his various positions are generally in accord with the received tradition, the major outlines may be stated.

One traditional question was whether full independence could be conceded by a ruler to particular subjects. Italian cities, for example, had claimed independent status by virtue of concessions from the Emperor. According to Bodin, any concession of this sort is an extreme alienation of domain, and, in principle at least, is forbidden absolutely:

Thus it was not in the power of the Emperors, or of any prince whatever, to alienate any part of the public domain, and least of all the rights of sovereign majesty, without it being always in the power of his successor to lay hands on it, just as a master may always retake his fugitive slave.[23]

Another and more difficult issue was whether the kingdom as a whole, or even a portion of the kingdom, could be ceded to a foreign prince either as an outright transfer or, more commonly, in the form of feudal dependency. For Bodin, the existence or non-existence of a restriction is made to depend on the specific character of the law of succession to the throne.

In kingships like the French, the consent of the community was needed for transfer of the kingdom as a whole, since the alienation would violate the Salic law. By somewhat more complicated reasoning, the prohibition of the Salic law would also prevent alienation of a portion of the kingdom without the consent of its lord, if not of its inhabitants. The transfer of a vassal without his own consent would violate the ruler's obligation to protect him.[24] It could not be accomplished by the ruler legally unless he were also entitled to transfer the kingship as a whole with all its rights and obligations, and this, as we have seen, is forbidden by the Salic law, unless of course the whole community consents:

And on this account it was decided that Philip the Fair, King of France, could not make Arthur, Duke of Brittany, the vassal of the King of England, against the wishes of the Duke, unless he [Philip] were to leave his entire kingdom to the King of England. But this he could not do without the consent of the Estates – and not even by his absolute authority despite what some have said.[25]

[23] *Ibid.* p. 182 (129).
[24] The use of feudal notions to develop a general obligation to protect is traced to Baldus by Peter N. Riesenberg, *Inalienability of Sovereignty in Medieval Political Thought* (New York, 1956) p. 136. Bodin's formulation follows this tradition and, perhaps for this reason, is more cautious and more narrowly feudal than some of the larger and more eloquent conceptions beginning to be developed in the period. Thus, Hotman, *Quaestiones illustres* (1573) in *Operum*, II, pp. 847ff; and, slightly earlier, Fernando Vazquez de Menchaca (Vasquius), *Controversiarum illustrium . . . libri tres* (1564) (Valladolid, 1931), I, 4 (vol. I, pp. 148–9).
[25] *République*, I, 9, p. 179 (127).

According to Barclay, as we have noted,[26] extreme violation of this rule would justify preventive action on the part of the community. But this was not a problem that Bodin considered. He simply assumed that transfers made without consent were liable to subsequent recovery, which seemed adequate for all his purposes. The French public had some protection against permanent divisions of the realm through hasty actions by the kings, while the kings, in turn, were given a convenient pretext for repudiating cessions by their predecessors on the grounds that due procedures were omitted. It may also be noted that all of this would apply to elective kingships too, although Bodin neglects to point this out.

On the other hand, for ' hereditary ' kingships like the Spanish or the English, this protection is specifically denied.[27] An hereditary kingship, for Bodin, seems to have been one in which the law of succession to the crown was substantially the same as the law of intestate succession to private property, and in which the incumbent was perhaps technically entitled to vary the order of succession by his testament as long as he confined his choice to a member of the ruling family.[28] In such kingships the ' cause ' which established the right of a successor lay, as it were, in the progenitor. In ' successive ' kingships, on the other hand, of which the sole exemplar would seem to be the French, the ' cause ' of the successor's right was designation by a special public custom. One operational distinction between the first form of kingship and the second was whether women were permitted to succeed. In Spain and England, where the succession of women was permitted, succession to the throne seemed to follow the law of private inheritance. In France, on the other hand, the normal order of private inheritance was clearly overridden by the Salic law.

This distinction, which Bodin frequently invokes, was old in continental jurisprudence. French publicists, writing in the early 1400s, had rejected the concept of inheritance in order to protect the crown from various treaties on succession arising from the Hundred Years War.[29] By Bodin's time it was a commonplace of legal thought that a king of France, like the king of an elective monarchy, held his crown by public designation rather than hereditary right.

For some commentators, one consequence of this principle was that successors to the crown of France, unlike successors by inheritance, were not automatically obliged by the contracts and engagements of their predecessors.[30] This is the position that Bodin employs to deny the alienability of sovereignty in France. On the other hand, in Spain or England the king was not only

---

[26] See above, note 17. [27] *République*, 1, 9, p. 179 (127).
[28] See note 31 below.
[29] For the development of the legal theory, see Ralph E. Giesey, *The Juristic Basis of Dynastic Right to the French Throne* (Philadelphia, 1961) *passim* and especially pp. 12ff on Jean de Terre Rouge, who was the key figure in the formulation of the legal doctrine. See also Lemaire, *Lois fondamentales*, pp. 54ff, and F. Olivier-Martin, *Histoire du droit français* (Paris, 1948) p. 310. [30] See below, pp. 8off.

entitled to cede a portion of the kingdom to a foreigner, but could even transfer his entire realm, as in doing homage to a foreign prince. If an engagement were made, the successor to the crown was obligated. Since the kingship was a mere inheritance, consent of the Estates was not required.

It is hard to say exactly why Bodin insisted on this latter point. One possible motive, suggested by the context, was to show that the king of France enjoyed a security of title that no other king could claim. He may also have felt that the conclusion was imposed upon him by the logic of a traditional distinction.[31]

In any event, the result seems hopelessly inadequate. The rule was obviously unworkable, since no king of Spain or England could be realistically expected to acknowledge it, and even from a theoretical standpoint, it was inconsistent with other things that Bodin held. He believed, for example, that the kings of Spain or England were not entitled to alienate domain to subjects except in

---

[31] For clarification of this highly complicated technical distinction, see Giesey, *Dynastic Right*, *passim*, as well as Grotius, *Law of War and Peace*, II, 7, pp. 267ff, and Pufendorf, *Law of Nature*, VII, 7, pp. 1093ff. But, in order to indicate what it is that Bodin is confused about, a few very condensed observations may be offered here.

In Grotius and Pufendorf three main types of succession (other than election) are distinguished – patrimonial succession, in which the choice of a successor is left to the discretion of the incumbent and in which the rule of intestate succession is followed where the incumbent has made no designation; hereditary succession, in which the order of succession is legally fixed according to degree of proximity to the deceased incumbent; and successive kingship (or simple succession), in which the order of succession is legally fixed by lineal relationship to a remote progenitor of the dynasty. Lineal succession may either be cognate lineal succession (of which Castile is offered as the main example) or agnate lineal succession (which is the French rule of primogeniture through the male line only).

The theoretical distinction between fixed and patrimonial succession is simple enough, but the difference between hereditary and lineal succession is subtle and uncertain. From one standpoint, lineal succession is merely a more precise determination of the proximity of kinship relations to the incumbent and thus partakes of heredity. But from another standpoint, the successor by heredity is more like a private heir who, in Roman law, was a substitute for his predecessor in all aspects, while the lineal successor was more like the successor to a public office by election or appointment.

Bodin's confusions thus appear to be twofold. He does not distinguish clearly between patrimonial and hereditary – in part perhaps because the theory of succession was less well-developed in foreign countries. England, which Bodin believed to be hereditary, is a good example, at least in the fifteenth and early sixteenth centuries. He was, furthermore, unable to see the fundamental similarity in the legal status of hereditary and successive kings. He fails to see that the right of the heir in a system of fixed inheritance precludes the incumbent from alienating sovereignty or a portion of the sovereignty to another. He also fails to see that an heir whose right is fixed by law, need not be regarded as a strictly private heir and might thus be relieved of some of the obligations imposed on heirs by private law. In Grotius and Pufendorf both of these points are resolved in favor of the hereditary successor. It is assumed by these writers that in hereditary kingships, as distinguished from patrimonial kingships, the right of incumbents to dispose of the succession by testament was eliminated by a public law which was imposed by the community at the time the kingship was instituted. It is also assumed that by this same law the community intended, and tacitly provided, that successors in the kingship should not be required to assume all the obligations of a private heir but only those obligations consistent with their public duties. On this latter assumption the status of an hereditary king is fully assimilated to that of a successive king.

situations of emergency, and it is hard to see how this could be reconciled with the possibility of ceding sovereignty to foreigners. There is no reason, given Bodin's principles, why the successor should be exempt from the engagements of his predecessor in the first case but obligated in the second.

Bodin, then, would have been better advised to treat succession to the crown of Spain or England in the same fashion as succession to the crown of France – as a designation arising from the law according to a rule of consanguinity. This would not only have removed the inconsistency; it would also have been more congenial to his general perspective.

But apart from this aberration, his views on fundamental law seem adequate. His interpretation of the law of succession and the law of domain, and his application of these rules to the inalienability of sovereignty, are broadly consistent with French and European norms. The rules are logically consistent since they are all derived from the concept of the kingship as a life-estate. And they are also compatible with absolutism in Bodin's meaning of that term.

The law of nature, as we have often pointed out, was not regarded by Bodin as an obligation of the ruler which the community was entitled to enforce. It was essentially a moral obligation binding solely on the ruler's conscience. But this is not to say that he looked upon the law of nature as an insignificant restraint. He obviously believed that the rule of justice was so inherent in the entire order of human and natural relationships that it could not be persistently defied without disastrous consequences. Nor did he think that the law of nature was completely unprotected institutionally. There were many ways anticipated in which the magistrates and judges of a kingdom could impose limitations on a king without resorting to overt defiance or inviting armed resistance. The law of nature was thus a force in social life, and it seemed important to Bodin to define its injunctions with precision.

In most of its aspects, the law of nature was inherently variable in application. As a guide to legislation, the specific meaning of the rule of justice depended on the circumstances.[32] As a guide to execution, or rule of fair procedure in criminal and civil proceedings,[33] it could vary greatly with the form of state. Less variable were rights of private property and claims related to that right. These were substantive restrictions on the state traditionally supposed to be universal and definite in content, and Bodin was thus required to define their basis and their scope.

The two main obligations on the ruler, both well-established in the civil law tradition, were to honor contracts made with private subjects (as well as contracts made with foreign princes) and to recognize a claim for compensation where he had done damage to the right of property either inadvertently or by invocation of eminent domain. If Bodin put somewhat greater emphasis on

---

[32] *République*, i, 8, pp. 151–2 (105–6). [33] *Ibid*. vi, 6, pp. 1029–30 (768).

the obligation of contracts, it is in part because the issues were more complicated, and in part also because he was anxious to forestall misunderstanding.
Having held that engagements by a ruler to maintain existing law were not
completely binding, he could have been taken to imply that every royal contract was liable to the same flexibility. He wished, therefore, to make it very
clear that flexibility did not apply to contracts made with private individuals
to pay for loans, services, or goods from the general resources of the treasury.

The general obligation of the ruler to honor contracts of this sort was so well-
established in the civilian-canonist tradition that argument was hardly needed.
There were, however, points of controversy on interpretation. On one opinion,
which Bodin attributes to the canonists, the ruler's obligation by a contract
came solely from the law of nature, and was therefore less precise and binding
than the obligation of private parties under civil law, from which the ruler was
exempt. On this issue, Bodin adopts the stronger view, which seems to have
been taken by most of the civilians. Either the law of nature is as binding as
civil law in this respect, or else this is one respect in which the king, by virtue
of the law of nature, is bound by civil law.[34]

One other and more complicated question was the obligation of successor
kings to honor contracts entered into by their predecessors. The civilians of
the late thirteenth and early fourteenth centuries had been reticent and
cautious on this point. But they seem generally to have assumed that a
successor to the kingship was in much the same position as an heir in private
law. In assuming the status of his predecessor, he assumed the latter's
obligations.[35]

There were, however, certain obvious defects in this point of view. On the
theoretical level, the concept of inheritance could not be easily applied to elective kingships like the Empire. In its practical implications, the rule (in principle at least) gave no protection to the successor against irresponsible contracts
on the part of an incumbent or against claims that might arise from an
incumbent's frauds and delicts.

More congenial for Bodin's concerns, therefore, was a more sophisticated
line of reasoning that seems to have begun with Baldus. Distinguishing elective and successive princes, Baldus had contended that the latter only were
obligated directly by their predecessors, since it was from the predecessors
that office was acquired. The former, on the other hand – who received their
office from the public – could be obligated through the public only. In other
words, the incumbent to an elective kingship could bind his successor by a
contract only insofar as he could bind the public or the public treasury. The
test, accordingly, was whether the incumbent was acting ' in pursuance of his
dignity ', – that is, in his public role as distinguished from his purely personal
capacity. There was one condition, however, on which even his frauds and

[34] *Ibid*. I, 8, p. 153 (107).   [35] Carlyle and Carlyle, *Medieval Political Theory*, VI, p. 16.

delicts could give rise to continuing obligations. If his misbehavior had actually enriched the public treasury, the successor, as the public's steward, was bound to honor claims for restitution. The public, and the king, were forbidden by the law of nature to profit from another's loss.[36]

By the sixteenth century, Baldus' treatment of elective kingship had been gradually extended to successive monarchies as well,[37] and in Bodin's work, the assimilation is unusually bold and clear.[38] Given the prevailing interpretation of the Salic law, theoretical grounds were readily available. Since the kings of France did not acquire office from their predecessors, but were designated by a public law, they could be said to have the same position with respect to contracts as that of an elective king. They could not be bound by an obligation of their predecessors unless it had been contracted for a public purpose or stemmed from enrichment of the treasury.[39]

Curiously enough, the protection of this rule was also extended to 'hereditary' kingships like the Spanish and the English. At least on this topic – although not, as we have seen, in other contexts [40] – Bodin was willing to treat the usual order of succession in these systems as designations by a customary rule. Hence the only case in which the successor was completely bound was where he had actually received his kingdom by a testament.[41] There was one exception even here. Where a testament existed, and the person named was the designee of custom also, he could claim his title by the latter rule if he saw fit, and escape the obligations of a private heir. Such was the position of Edward VI, Mary, and Elizabeth I of England, all of whom came to the throne by the normal order of succession but had also been named in the testament of their father, Henry VIII. ' In this case ', says Bodin:

We must decide whether the designated heir wishes to accept the state in the capacity of heir or, renouncing the legacy of the testator, wishes to claim the crown by virtue of the custom and law of the land. In the first case the successor is bound by

---

[36] *Consilia sive responsa* (Venice, 1575) III, *cons.* 159, fos 45r–6r; and see also I, *cons.* 271, fos 81v–2r. The ramifications of these two *consilia*, and especially III, 159, are extremely rich. For wider commentary, see Ernst H. Kantorowicz, *The King's Two Bodies* (Princeton, 1957) pp. 398ff.

[37] But as late as the turn of the fifteenth century, Jason de Maino distinguished the rule of Baldus as applying only to elective kingships. Jason, apparently worried by the rule, claims with some relief that it cannot apply to a successive monarch : ' But . . . where kingdoms are transferred by succession, in the sense that the oldest son succeeds to the kingdom, duchy, or county, then, I think that, in so far as it is not incompatible with the general custom, the successor is bound to honor every compact and any agreement whatever just as if he were a private successor.' Commentary on *Digest*, I, 4, I, Jason de Maino, *In Primam Digesti Veteris Partem commentaria* (Venice, 1589) f. 23v.
On the other hand, Baldus himself, at least in the two *consilia* we have mentioned, does not draw the line this sharply, and may have envisaged an extension of the principle.

[38] Unusual in Bodin is his willingness to state, without evasion, that purely personal obligations do not continue. Cf. Rebuffi, comm. on *Digest*, I, I, 31, *Explicatio ad quatuor Pandectarum libros* (1549) (Lyon, 1589), p. 35, and Gregory of Toulouse, *De republica libri sex et viginti* (1596) (Frankfurt, 1609) 7, 20, 39, p. 312.   [39] *République*, I, 8, pp. 159–60 (111–12).

[40] See above, pp. 77–8.   [41] *République*, I, 8, p. 159 (111).

the acts and promises of his predecessor, as is any private heir. But in the second case he is not bound to the acts even if he [the predecessor] swore to them. For the predecessor's oath does not bind the successor, but the successor is bound to anything that may have turned to the kingdom's profit.[42]

The ' public ' theory of successor obligations was thus extended almost universally. The only problem was to determine which of the predecessor's acts were purely personal, and which were genuinely public. This was not a problem that Bodin took lightly. Although he wanted to protect successors from capricious charges, he was intensely aware that continuity of lawfully contracted obligations was essential to the public credit. Repudiation of debts was sternly disapproved as a means of restoring fiscal solvency.[43]

From this standpoint the test of advantage to the public treasury was obviously too permissive as applied to public contracts. A potential creditor could have little assurance by this rule, since he could never tell, at the time he made a contract, whether it would turn out to the advantage of the treasury or if it did whether it would be so regarded by successor kings. Looked at from the other side, the test of advantage to the public could work a serious hardship on the state. A king who had a need to borrow would be seriously handicapped by his inability to pledge the public faith conclusively.

Either responding to this problem or else attempting to ensure justice for the creditor, Baldus had suggested a procedural solution. If the incumbent, in entering a contract, should specifically declare that he intended his successors to be bound, or that he was acting in the name of the state, he could thereby indicate that his act was being done in his public capacity and that the faith of the public was engaged.[44] There is some indication of a similar notion in Bodin, but, understandably enough, it is not a thought that he pursued. If the incumbent's declaration had always to be taken on its face, the successor could be bound too easily. Later writers would consider the incumbent's words as a presumptive indication of honest and reasonable intent, but would refuse to regard it as absolutely definitive.[45] Bodin achieves a similar result by holding that any engagement is binding on successors if the consequence is not too prejudicial.[46]

There was, however, one alternative which Bodin explores with respect to the validity of treaties. Observing that treaties by the king of France are subject to the same conditions of extinction as any of his other contracts, he holds that these limitations can be overcome if the treaty is publicly ratified:

If, then, the sovereign prince has made an engagement in his capacity as sovereign on a matter that concerns the state and profits it, the successors are bound. And much more are they bound if the agreement (*traicté*) was made with the consent of

---

[42] *Ibid*. p. 159 (112).   [43] *Ibid*. vi, 2, p. 896 (676). And see below p. 83.

[44] Baldus, *Consilia*, iii, 159, fos 45v–46r.

[45] Thus Grotius, *Law of War and Peace*, ii, 14, 12, p. 387, and Pufendorf, *Law of Nature*, viii, 10, 8, p. 1346.   [46] *République*, i, 8, pp. 160–1 (113).

the Estates, or the principal towns and communities, or the Parlements, or the princes and most eminent nobles. They [the successors] would then be bound even if the agreement (*traicté*) was disadvantageous to the public in view of the [pledged] faith and obligation of the subjects.[47]

Public ratification thus transforms the successors' obligation from a mere obligation not to profit from another's loss, if the agreement should prove advantageous, into one that is fully and strictly contractual. The idea, moreover, was potentially wider in its applications. Although Bodin is thinking mainly, and perhaps exclusively, of treaties, the notion could apply to contracts with a private subject through the usual procedure of verification by the Parlements. Bodin perhaps was using a similar idea when he insisted on public ratification to validate alienations of domain. In both situations the effect of ratification is to debar the successor from refusing to acknowledge the result.

The only difficulty with this solution is to explain the binding effect of public ratification. To say, as Bodin does, that the ' faith and obligation of the subjects ' is entailed might tend to compromise the principle of absolutism. For if the pledge of the public is decisive, it must be entitled to fulfill its obligation even against the wishes of the king. Perhaps Bodin should have said that solemn consultation of the public by the king gives clear indication that he deliberately and responsibly intends to act in his public capacity. The approval of the Estates or other body would be an attestation of this serious intent, and the result would be a modified and closely guarded version of Baldus' suggestion on solemn declarations.

Having thus indicated the rationale and qualifications of Bodin's rule on the obligation of successors, it is well to let him state them for himself:

But if the prince has contracted with a foreigner, or even with a subject on some matter of interest to the public, without the consent of those whom I have mentioned, then if the contract is highly prejudicial to the public, his successor in the state is not bound in any way, and all the less so if he succeeds by right of election. In that case one cannot say that he holds anything by virtue of his predecessor, as would be the case if he had come into the state by way of a gift (*résignation*). But if the acts of his predecessor have turned to the profit of the public, the successor is always bound by them, no matter in what capacity he takes the throne. Otherwise, he would be permitted to derive profit from another's loss by fraud or deviousness, and the commonwealth could perish in its time of need since no one would be willing to give aid, which result is against equity and natural reason.[48]

This passage, taken together with the others we have cited, form a rule of obligation that is designed to give every possible protection to the creditor, short of holding that every obligation of a king is permanently binding. Where

---

[47] *Ibid*. p. 160 (113).
[48] *Ibid*. pp. 160–1 (113). The special reference to elective kingship in this passage is not intended to be juridically restrictive. It is simply language carried over from the Italian civilians from whom Bodin derived his conceptual scheme.

ratification has occurred the right of the creditor or holder of alienated domain
is fully guaranteed. Even without ratification, the right of the creditor is
guaranteed if the result of the agreement was advantageous to the public.
Bodin seems also to be suggesting that the contract may be binding on successors even where the outcome was unfavourable, if the engagement was
solemnly made and the result was not too prejudicial. In every case, moreover,
a lawful engagement is fully binding on the king who undertook it.

At the same time none of these rules (with the slight exception we have mentioned) is incompatible with absolute authority as Bodin understood it. Engagements entered into by incumbents are binding solely through the law of
nature and not by consent of the community. Where consent is used to ensure
the obligation of successors, it is permissive and corroborative rather than
restrictive, and the right corroborated is that of the creditor, not of the community. The successor, finally, is not directly or immediately obligated by any
act of the community or even by the act of his predecessor. He is obligated only
indirectly by his ' natural ' duty to do justice and maintain the public credit.
At no point, therefore, does the public have a right to act against him.

The security of private property against arbitrary seizure by the state, either
by expropriation without a lawful pretext, or by taking for a public use without compensation to the owner, was overwhelmingly, if not quite universally,
accepted in the civil law tradition. On a very literal reading of the phrase
omnia principis esse (everything is the prince's) in *Code* 7, 37, 3, some of the
glossators had maintained that the Emperor held title to all property. But in
the main tradition the standard reply to his interpretation was Seneca's celebrated maxim: ' The king holds everything by public power, but ownership
is in the hands of individuals (*omnia rex imperio possidet, singuli dominio*).' [49]

Bodin enthusiastically repeats this maxim as a defining norm of ' royal
monarchy ' [50] and then insists that royal monarchy is virtually required by the
law of nature. Systems in which the king is truly the proprietor of everything
are called lordly or despotic monarchies, and their legitimacy is cast in doubt.[51]
In the European tradition, the idea of an ' oriental ' kingship, in which the
ruler had legal title to the persons and the possessions of his subjects, had
always been treated as inherently uncivilized.[52] According to Bodin, despotic
monarchy, like slavery, was a derogation from the law of nature usually
arising from an act of conquest. But it was a practice that had occurred so

---

[49] Nicolini, *La proprietá*, pp. 107ff.　　　　　　[50] *République*, 1, 8, p. 157 (110).

[51] In the *Methodus*, the states thus classified together are distinguished from the other class of
monarchies because their rulers are above the law in general. The basis of demarcation has
thus been significantly narrowed. See above, pp. 36–7. Bodin now refers to the despotic
form as ' seigneurial ', or ' lordly ', to suggest the parallel with ownership of private
property. The despotic king ' has ' everything not only by *imperium*, but also by
dominium as well.

[52] For a succinct and lucid history of the concept of despotism as used by political thinkers from
the Greeks to the middle of the nineteenth century, see Melvin Richter, ' The History of the
Concept of Despotism ', *Dictionary of the History of Ideas* (forthcoming).

often and had been accepted by so many peoples that he was not prepared to condemn it absolutely. It had to be regarded as something tolerated by the law of peoples.[53] Yet in admitting its legitimacy, Bodin observes that it is a kind of power that is liable to abuse, and that it is associated with barbaric times or places.

He is thus at pains to show that despotic title is absent in European kingships, and ought not to be inferred from the formal status of the king as feudal overlord. He is willing to concede that the barbarian invaders of the Roman Empire established some semblance of despotic power. But they did so only partially, since they did not claim all the land, and usually respected the liberty of persons. As manners softened in the course of time, even this limited lordship was formerly restricted:

And it might be said that there is no monarch in Europe who does not claim direct lordship over all his subjects' goods, and that there is no individual who does not acknowledge that he holds his goods of the sovereign prince. But I say that this does not suffice to hold that the monarchy is lordly, in view of the fact that the subject is avowed by the prince as a true proprietor who may dispose of his goods, while the prince had only feudal lordship according to law (*droite seigneurie*). Besides there are many allodial holdings where he has neither property nor feudal lordship according to the law.[54]

Hence in all European kingdoms, there were rights of private property, not excluding possessions held in fief. Where these existed, the right of property could not be taken without violation of the law of nature. The sole exception to this rule, apart from punishments for crime,[55] was the taking of property for public use, where the public need was evident and where compensation was provided or promised. That the individual could be required to yield his property where public necessity demanded, was a well-established doctrine, and Bodin would probably have accepted most of the cases of necessity that were defined in the civil law tradition. Yet he appears reluctant to be too permissive. Only one example of public need is actually mentioned – defeat in war where confiscation of property is necessary in order to conclude a peace. But even then, compensation must be paid the owner, since the public may not profit from a member's loss. This requirement, although common in the juridical tradition, was not unanimous, and Bodin, insisting on this, is aware that he is rejecting opinion to the contrary.[56]

Within certain limits, it was also possible to hold that all these obligations of the ruler could be cited against him in the courts. Access to the courts for suits against the sovereign was a prominent feature of the French tradition to

---

[53] *République*, II, 2, pp. 273–4 (200–1), pp. 278–9 (203–4). On the legitimacy of slavery, which Bodin is even more reluctant to admit, see I, 5.

[54] *Ibid*. II, 2, p. 275 (201–2).

[55] Leaving aside of course such special rights of confiscation as the *droit d'aubaine* by which the inheritance of an unnaturalized foreigner passed to the sovereign. See *ibid*. I, 6, p. 94ff (65f).   [56] *Ibid*. I, 8, p. 157 (109).

which Bodin was much attracted. He even says that royal obligations are more rigorously construed in such proceedings than those of ordinary subjects. If the king should fail to answer through his procurators, no delay is granted and the verdict is awarded to the plaintiff. In disputes arising from a royal contract, the performance required of a king is more precise than what would be demanded of a private party, on the grounds that the king should be the exemplar of good faith.[57]

But the power of the courts to examine suits against the king becomes incompatible with absolute authority if carried to its logical extreme, and there are certain limitations on the power that Bodin mentions or implies. The power, to begin with, is a privilege rather than a right, since it is held only on the ruler's sufferance.[58] The king, no doubt, has an inherent obligation to do justice, and is required by the law of nature to grant some sort of hearing, either by himself or by his agents. But he is not required to give a magistrate the power to hear or to decide.

Even where the power is accorded and the verdict goes against the ruler, he is technically able to ignore it with impunity, since his person cannot be constrained. ' [T]he person of the sovereign is always excepted in civil law, no matter what power and authority he gives another; and he never gives so much to anyone, that he does not keep more himself '.[59] Or, to put it in yet another way, the presence of the sovereign utterly extinguishes the power of the magistrate and momentarily returns him to the status of a private person vis-à-vis the ruler.[60] If the verdict of an authorized hearing was defied without good cause, the king would be culpable of tyranny according to the law of nature. But the common law provides no remedy for this infraction.

We turn now to the final and most puzzling of Bodin's limitations, which is his rule on new taxation. In the course of arguing that the kings of England may legislate without consent, he pauses to consider the objection that this would not apply to new taxation:

But someone may say that the Estates [of England] do not suffer any imposition of extraordinary charges or subsidies unless they have been accorded and consented to in Parliament pursuant to the ordinance of Edward I in the great charter [Magna Carta?] by virtue of which the people have always prevailed against the kings. I reply that other kings have no more power than the king of England, because there is not a prince in all the world who has it in his power to levy taxes on subjects at his pleasure, any more than he has the power to take another's property, as Philippe de Commines wisely admonished at the Estates of Tours according to his *Mémoires*. Nevertheless, if the necessity is urgent, the prince should not wait for the Estates to assemble, or for the consent of the people, since

[57] *Ibid.* p. 153 (106–7), p. 158 (111).
[58] *Ibid.* p. 130 (90).
[59] *Ibid.* p. 123 (85).
[60] *Ibid.* p. 127 (88).

their safety depends on the foresight and diligence of a wise prince. But we will speak of this in its proper place.[61]

Leaving aside for the moment the qualification included in the penultimate sentence of this passage, the basic rule is incompatible with absolute authority, although Bodin of course was not aware of this. He apparently believed that consent to new taxation was no more incompatible with absolutism than consent to alienation of domain or ratification of a treaty or a contract.

But if this was his idea, he was mistaken. In the other situations we have treated, such as alienation of domain, the legal function of consent was to transform provisional arrangements into a permanent obligation binding on successors. Consent to new taxation, on the other hand, would be required for action in the present, and for this reason it violates the principle of absolutism. In this situation the requirement of consent denies the power of a sovereign to act without another's leave, and would thus imply a right of resistance on the part of the community if the procedures of consent were not observed. Nor is this consequence obviated by the fact that a king is not required to wait upon consent in an emergency. Since this is the exception rather than the rule, clear abuse of the emergency provision would also justify resistance.

There was perhaps a deeper inadvertence on Bodin's part that reassured him. He could have thought that the obligation to consult, being based upon the law of nature, was enforceable by God alone and could give no occasion for legitimate resistance. But this solution is equally unworkable. The law of nature, as Bodin habitually interprets it, is confined to substantive requirements, and from a substantive standpoint the most that could be said about taxes is that the king is forbidden to impose them unless there is a public need.[62] Hence procedures of consent would not derive directly from the law of nature. They would have to follow from an inherent right of the community independently established by history and custom.

This conclusion can also be looked at from another angle. If consent to taxation were indeed required by the law of nature, Bodin's entire position would be undermined. Since the test of a legitimate tax is the existence of a public need, the right of consent in the community is a right of determining that need. But according to the law of nature, the existence of a proper public need is one test for any act of government, and especially an act of legislation. Hence, the rule of consent to new taxation would have to be extended universally.

On the question of taxation, therefore, Bodin was inconsistent, and it is an especially surprising inconsistency since he went out of his way, as it were, to introduce it. The idea of consent to new taxation was not so emphatic in the

---

[61] *Ibid.* p. 140 (96–7). The passage is partly inspired by Comines, *Mémoires*, J. Calmette and G. Durville eds., 3 vols (Paris, 1965) II, pp. 217ff (V, ch. 19).

[62] This, of course, is the traditional view of the civilians. See, for example, the opinion of Bartolus quoted in Carlyle and Carlyle, *Medieval Political Theory*, VI, p. 77.

French tradition that Bodin had special need to depart from his absolutist doctrine in order to acknowledge it. In medieval thought the basic attitude toward royal taxes was that they should not exist at all, since, in principle at least, the king was expected to live upon his own. Where new taxation was required for abnormal purposes, the need for consent was assumed and often stated.[63] But this idea had never been given the degree of institutional embodiment it was destined to receive in England. There was no clear parallel in France to a national body like the English Parliament, which habitually granted new taxation and insisted on that privilege as one condition for the perpetuation of its other powers. The Parlement of Paris had rarely attempted to assume that role, and the French Estates had never had the unity and continuity to explore that course persistently.

The French constitutionalist tradition, therefore, had not put special emphasis on consent to new taxation.[64] Insofar as consent was understood as a requirement, it was a mere implication of consent to legislation generally. Ironically enough, this failure to distinguish taxation as a special issue was also characteristic of Bodin's earlier work. At one point in the *Methodus* he considers, but tentatively rejects, the proposition that the power to tax is a prerogative of sovereignty.[65] But this has nothing to do with any special insistence on consent. It is simply a hesitant concession, later taken back,[66] that the ruler's power of taxation may be shared with other magistrates and local corporations. The question of consent is never taken up specifically.

In the *République*, accordingly, Bodin could have treated the levying of taxes like any other act of legislation. He could have said that consent was desirable and usual, but was not constitutionally required. And he could have supported this position by pointing to many exceptions from consent in France – and in England too, no doubt, had he seriously attempted to discover instances. We must assume, accordingly, that his insistence on consent to new taxation was the result of strong political motivations of a special sort.

Before attempting to explain this purpose, one other *caveat* seems useful. Bodin's motivations would not be correctly understood if constitutionalist objectives are imputed. Taken out of context, his rule of consent to new taxation might seem to intend a far-reaching role for the Estates. It might seem to envisage the use of this right by the Estates to extract institutional

---

[63] Comines, *Mémoires*, v, 19.

[64] Even in the Huguenots, it has no special prominence. The *Francogallia* barely touches on it, and *Vindiciae contra tyrannos* is brief. See Franklin, *Constitutionalism and Resistance*, pp. 60, 76.

[65] *Methodus*, p. 175 (173).

[66] *République*, I, 10, p. 244 (177). Bodin now says that taxes may be imposed and repealed by the sovereign 'alone'. But this is not incompatible with the requirement of consent in I, 8, p. 140 (96–7) and elsewhere. 'Alone' in this context means to the exclusion of other magistrates. The king 'alone' could ask the Estates for permission to enact. The verbal difficulties here will exemplify the kind of caution needed in reading 'absolutist' statements dating from this period.

concessions. This interpretation of his motives might seem to be corroborated by Bodin's own behavior at the Estates of Blois. It would thus appear that he was after all a secret constitutionalist. For, in view of the chronic imbalance of the royal budget and the near exhaustion of public credit, the government had become increasingly dependent upon new taxation. The crown, in a period of weakness, had been forced to assemble the Estates, and at each of the assemblies between 1560 and 1576 the Estates had attempted to make use of their financial leverage to encroach upon the crown's prerogatives. Bodin, in insisting on consent to new taxation, might thus appear to be endorsing such attempts.

But this appearance is misleading. The truth rather is that Bodin's purposes were purely fiscal and were utterly innocent of any grand constitutional design.[67] We have seen that he, like most contemporaries, was fully convinced that the king could and should live of his own – that the income from domain, in other words, was potentially sufficient to defray the costs of government. According to a recent reckoning, almost the entire domain had already been rented at a mere fraction of its market value. Had the rents been realistic, the yield, according to Bodin, would be 3,000,000 *livres* annually, which was enough not only to maintain the royal household but to pay the salaries of public officers without dipping into the return from ordinary and extra-ordinary imposts.[68] It followed, therefore, that the only sensible solution to the existing fiscal crisis was to redeem the domain by paying compensation to its holders, and to re-rent it at profitable levels and with adequate safeguards. To gather money for repurchase some new taxation might be needed, but almost everything could be accomplished by better management of the income from existing sources. If the king abstained from lavish gifts to favorites, suppressed unnecessary offices, and removed inefficiency and corruption in collections of his income,[69] funds could be accumulated for redemption of the crown's domain, and the burden of taxation, far from being raised, could be gradually reduced.[70]

These calculations were surely much too optimistic, but Bodin was probably right in his beliefs that without a solution of this sort the monarchy was ultimately doomed. It seemed to him that the burden of taxation was already intolerably high and utterly absurd, especially when measured by the English level. Were the burden to be raised still higher, rebellion must result. In his chapter on finances the king is constantly reminded that revolutions are more frequently caused by high taxation than by any other grievance.

---

[67] A fine treatment of Bodin's political and economic objectives, which also surveys previous attempts to explain the contradiction in his thought, is Martin Wolfe, 'Jean Bodin on Taxes: The Sovereignty-Taxes Paradox', *Political Science Quarterly*, LXXXIII, no. 2, June 1968, pp. 268–84.

[68] *République*, VI, 2, pp. 862–3 (654).

[69] *Ibid*. pp. 901 (679), 903–5 (681–2), 908–9 (684).   [70] *Ibid*. p. 882 (666).

We may thus assume that Bodin's insistence on consent was designed to make new taxation as difficult as possible without excluding it entirely. Since new taxation might be needed temporarily to redeem the crown domain, and might otherwise be necessary in a time of dire need, Bodin is bound to acknowledge its legitimacy. But in view of the attendant dangers, he wishes to make sure that the power will not be used too frequently. Hence he introduces the consent of the Estates as a limiting condition. Since the Estates were notoriously hostile to taxation, they would not be likely to indulge a king's requests unless the need was evident and taxation was the only remedy.[71]

The rule of consent to new taxation was therefore intended as a kind of 'fundamental' and quasi-automatic limitation on the fiscal power of the state itself. Bodin did not anticipate that the Estates would use the right to bind the power of the king in other areas of public policy and thus alter the institutional relationships on which absolute authority was founded. From this perspective, consent to new taxation could well have seemed to be consistent with his general constitutional conception.

In certain situations, as Bodin probably knew, the powers of consent could have an indirect effect on royal policy. One consequence of his tenacious and successful resistance to grants of new taxation at the Estates of Blois, and to alienations of domain, was to make war against the Huguenots more difficult. He was surely cognizant of this connection, and could hardly have been disapproving. But at no point was he prepared to countenance the use of fiscal leverage, or of any other resource of the Estates, to enhance their institutional position, even though an opportunity was offered that led, or seemed to lead, in this direction.

Almost from the very beginning of the Estates of Blois, proposals had been made for participation by the Estates in the preparation of the royal ordinance which the king, in accordance with tradition, would issue in answer to the *cahiers* and which would not be published until after the Estates had been dissolved. Among other features of the scheme was the appointment of a commission of thirty-six deputies, twelve from each of the three Estates, to collaborate with the Privy Council in passing judgment on the *cahiers*. Henry III, eager to gain support for subsidies, evasively agreed to go along.[72]

---

[71] Commenting on the ruinous consequences of public distributions in ancient republics, Bodin observes: ' That does not occur in a monarchy, since monarchs – who have no revenue more assured than that from the domain, and who have no right to tax their subjects without consent except in cases of urgent necessity – are not so prodigal with their domain.' *Ibid.* p. 863 (655).

[72] Jean Bodin, *Recueil de tout ce qui s'est négocié en la compagnie du tiers-état de France en l'assemblée générale des trois états, assigné par le roi en la ville de Blois au 15 novembre 1576*, in C.-H. Mayer; *Des États généraux et autres assemblées nationales* (Paris and The Hague, 1788) XIII (pp. 212–328), p. 223. Henry would have limited the commissioners to a purely advisory role, and he also rejected the proposal that all grievances unanimously accepted by all three of the Estates should be adopted automatically.

Bodin, however, was bitterly and adamantly opposed. Much of his concern was immediately political. He feared that the twelve deputies chosen from the Third – in a weak minority position – would be tempted to concede too much and might even approve alienations of domain. Where, moreover, the grievances of the Third were directed against the other two Estates, he evidently expected that the Third would be more likely to get satisfaction if the king alone passed judgment than if the points of difference were submitted to a joint commission.[73] But he also argued that the absolute power of the sovereign, which he takes to be a given, would turn the joint commission into a cruel and dangerous illusion. The king, he implied, might use the commission to advance his own designs. But the commission would be unable to control the king, since the sovereign, having absolute authority, could treat its advice as he saw fit.[74]

Hence Bodin's opposition as a deputy at Blois was devoid of constitutionalist intentions.[75] Although he boldly championed the right of the Estates to withhold requested subsidies, he never challenged the absolute power of the ruler in any other area of public policy. The purpose of his opposition was simply to protect the Third Estate from an unnecessary increase in the burden of taxation, and also to deter the king himself from a course of fiscal and religious policy that he believed to be politically disastrous.

Thus understood, Bodin's insistence on consent was apparently consistent with his desire for a strong and independent kingship. If he failed to see legal inconsistency, it was very likely because he could not think of new taxation as an ordinary function of the state. It seemed so abnormal and perverse to him that he could not assimilate it to the kinds of powers that monarchs properly exerted. Hence in requiring consent to new taxation he ignored the larger implication.

But this larger implication was quickly noticed by his near contemporaries whose doctrine of the state was broadly similar. In Gregory of Toulouse and William Barclay, consent to new taxation is reduced to a prudential maxim.[76] The ruler is earnestly reminded that consultation of the Estates is the course of wisdom and decency. But he is also told that, in principle at least, he is free to levy taxes on his own determination of the public need. It is this interpre-

---

[73] Owen Ulph, ' Jean Bodin and the Estates-General of 1576 ', *Journal of Modern History*, XIX, no. 4, December 1947 (pp. 289–96), pp. 295–6.

[74] *Recueil*, pp. 277–80.

[75] On two occasions [*République*, I, 8, p. 140 (97), III, 7, p. 501 (384)] Bodin remarks, incidentally, that the English Parliament usually meets more frequently than the Estates of other countries because the rule of consent to new taxation is there so well observed. It is just barely possible that he felt that emphasis on this rule for France would lead to a similar result, which he regarded as desirable (see below, p. 101). But beyond this he gives no indication of any political objective, and he would not have thought that more frequent Estates assemblies would alter the institutional relationships of king and Estates.

[76] Claude Collot, *L'École doctrinale de droit public de Pont-à-Mousson* (Paris, 1965) p. 179.

tation, rather than Bodin's, which was to become the standard opinion among legal commentators of the seventeenth century. In Charles Loyseau, for instance, Bodin's view is carefully excluded.[77]

Overall, however, Bodin's position was consistent. With the one exception of consent to new taxation, he admitted no limitation on the sovereign which the community could be entitled to enforce. He anticipated some situations in which the act of an incumbent, done without consent, would not be binding on successors. But even then, the act of the community was corroborative rather than preventive.

At the same time, the incumbent ruler had full and sole possession of all the powers that were ordinarily required for conduct of his government. In some situations – like the alienation of domain in time of war, or the levying of taxes for emergencies – his capacity to act would be enhanced by community support. But in Bodin's view at least, these exceptions were narrowly defined, and applied only to extraordinary situations.

This, then, is what he meant by absolute authority. An absolute king had full possession of all the powers that a state could legitimately exercise, and even if he overstepped the bounds of higher law, he could not be lawfully resisted or deposed.

[77] Charles Loyseau, *Traité des Seigneuries* (1610) ch. 3, pp. 14, 16, in *Oeuvres* (Lyon, 1701). This is a revised version of the first edition (1608) in which Loyseau was still somewhat hesitant. See Myron P. Gilmore, ' Authority and Property in the Seventeenth Century: the First Edition of the *Traité des Seigneuries* of Charles Loyseau ', *Harvard Library Bulletin*, IV (1950) no. 2 (pp. 258–65) p. 260.

CHAPTER 6

The Question of Resistance

Even if the sovereign should violate the law of nature and even if his violation should be blatant and habitual, his subjects were legally and morally enjoined from forcible resistance. This principle was not merely one among many conclusions for Bodin. It was, as we have tried to show, the implicit starting point on which his entire enterprise was founded. In his reinterpretation of European kingship he had constantly attempted to exorcise the right of resistance by the attribution of absolute authority, and in Book II, chapter 5, he simply spells out this consequence.

An absolute ruler obviously cannot be punished or controlled pursuant to law itself, for there is no one empowered to restrain him:

> For as to control by way of law (*voie de justice*), the subject has no jurisdiction over his prince, since it is from him that all power and authority to command derives, and not only may he revoke all the power and jurisdiction of every magistrate, but in his presence the power and jurisdiction of all magistrates, guilds and corporations, estates and communities, entirely lapses, as we have said.[1]

The absence of recourse in pursuance of law is thus an analytic implication of supremacy. To say that the Estates or magistrates are legally entitled to restrain is to define a monarchy like the German Empire or kingdom of Denmark, which, in Bodin's terminology, are principates. In these systems resistance is permitted to maintain the law, but only because the sovereignty resides in the Estates.[2] A monarchy, in other words, is either absolute and immune from resistance pursuant to law, or it is not a monarchy at all.

From Bodin's standpoint, resort to arms outside the law (*par voie de fait*) was also excluded by this argument. Resort to force outside the law must either be by public authorities beneath the king or else be allowed to private subjects generally. But to permit resistance by the magistrates would imply that the monarchy is limited, that the persons whom the king appoints to office are not reduced to the status of private subjects by his presence, and that they are thus possessed of an inherent power to constrain the king within the law as well. For Bodin, therefore, all resistance to a king outside the law must always be the act of private subjects, and this appears to be not only dangerous but almost inherently absurd. To legitimate resort to arms by way of fact within a legal order is virtually to contradict the very principle of legal

[1] *République*, II, 5, p. 302 (222).   [2] *Ibid.* pp. 301–2 (221–2).

order. The practical effect is to declare open season on monarchs good as well as bad, which is to invite degeneration into anarchy.[3]

This implication of the principle of sovereignty seemed explicitly confirmed by the common law of peoples. In every commonwealth resistance to supreme authority, or *lèse majesté*, is condemned and punished by the law.[4] In this respect, moreover, the arrangements made by men seemed fully supported by the higher law. They are corroborated by the law of God which forbids resistance to the higher powers.[5]

Bodin was uncomfortably aware that a different conclusion had been reached by reputable writers of the past. He was puzzled by the fact that St Thomas and other eminent authorities had admitted, or appeared to have admitted, that resistance might sometimes be legitimate even against sovereign authorities. The explanation, obviously, is that most of these writers were implicitly working with a concept of limited supremacy. But Bodin, ignoring this, could only dismiss their conclusions as anomalous.[6]

More congenial to his purposes was the position of Luther and Calvin, who drastically prohibited resistance on the part of ordinary subjects, and whose authority is therefore cited.[7] Calvin, of course, explicitly insisted on an exception to the rule of non-resistance for certain kinds of magistrates. 'For if ', he says,

there be, in the present day, any magistrates appointed for the protection of the people and the moderation of the power of kings, such as were, in ancient times, the Ephori, who were a check upon the kings among the Lacedaemonians, or the popular tribunes on the consuls among the Romans, or the Demarchi upon the senate among the Athenians; or with power such as perhaps is now possessed by the three estates in every kingdom when they are assembled; I am so far from prohibiting them, in the discharge of their duty, to oppose the violence or cruelty of kings, that I affirm that if they connive at kings in their oppression of their people, such forbearance involves the most nefarious perfidy because they fraudulently betray the liberty of the people, of which they know that they have been appointed protectors by the ordination of God.[8]

But these exceptions, of which Bodin was well aware, could be readily dismissed through the findings of his theory of sovereignty. Commenting

---

[3] *Ibid.* p. 307 (225). [4] *Ibid.* p. 303 (222–3).

[5] *Ibid.* pp. 303–6 (223–4). All of his scriptural citations are drawn from the Old Testament, which is an interesting confirmation of his theological tendencies.

[6] The list of writers is given at *ibid.* p. 300, n. 9 (not included in the English translation). The comment on this list (*ibid.* English, 220) is as follows: 'A number of doctors [of civil law] and theologians who have touched on this question have decided that it is permissible to kill a tyrant, and without distinction [as to the nature of the tyrant's title or the status of the persons resisting]. And some of them have even joined these two inconsistent words together and spoken of a "tyrant king", which has caused the ruin of fair and flourishing monarchies.' Bodin's uncertainty on this tradition appears obvious.

[7] *Ibid.* p. 306 (224–5), but especially p. 305, n. 2 (not included in English).

[8] *Institutes of the Christian Religion*, John Allen trans. (Grand Rapids, 1949) IV, ch. XXXI, p. 804.

upon Calvin's list, Bodin points out that the ephors of Sparta were the magistrates of a republic, since the kings were merely titular, and that their power to constrain the kings had nothing to do with power to constrain a sovereign. It was simply an example of resistance ' by way of law '. By the same reasoning it was even more obvious that the power of the Roman tribunes to control the consuls, or of the Athenian demarchs to control the senate, were not examples of legitimate resistance to a sovereign ' by way of fact '. The only problem, then, was the right of the Estates in European kingdoms, and the entire point of Bodin's constitutional doctrine was to show that in any monarchy worthy of the name there was no power of review or control in the Estates. He thus observes, laconically, that when Calvin comes to the ' ephoral ' powers of the Estates, ' he says " perhaps ", not daring to be definite '.[9]

Having thus established that resistance to a duly constituted king was always forbidden to his subjects, Bodin had accomplished his objective, and could be perfectly conventional, and sometimes even bold, on all the other principles traditionally associated with the doctrine of resistance. The protection of his rule of non-resistance, accordingly, is not extended to a mere usurper. Since the *tyrannus ex defectu tituli* has no title to exercise authority, he is no better than a common outlaw, and may be opposed or killed by anyone. The usurper who succeeds in stabilizing his authority can eventually acquire title either by express consent of the community or by passage of sufficient time. But Bodin is very strict on the requirements.[10]

Even in the other situation, where the title of the tyrant is legitimate, the rule of non-resistance is not extended to persons not properly his subjects.[11] The *tyrannus ab exercitio* may be corrected by a foreign prince,[12] and also

---

[9] *République*, II, 5, p. 306 (225).   [10] *Ibid.* pp. 298–9 (218–20).

[11] For one moment, in the introductory passage to II, 5 at p. 297 (298), Bodin seems inclined to restrict the term tyrant to usurper. See also note 6 above. But throughout II, 5, as well as in II, 4, on the character of tyranny, he constantly makes use of the traditional notion of a ' tyrant king ', i.e. of a ruler, legitimate by title, who has degenerated into tyrannical behavior in his exercise of power. It would appear that the point at II, 5, 297 is simply to suggest that the tyrant by usurpation is alone subject to resistance. He either has no title whatsoever, or, having a title inferior to that of sovereign, has illegally usurped complete authority.

[12] *Ibid.* II, 5, pp. 300 (220), 307 (225). The right of foreign intervention for outrages against the law of nature by a barbarian or tyrant was acknowledged in the Spanish school of natural law in the sixteenth century and would also be acknowledged by Grotius (*Law of War and Peace*, II, 20, 40, pp. 505–6). It does not seem incompatible with absolute authority over subjects, although Bodin does not elaborate. Since the principle had been adopted by the Huguenots (see Beza in Franklin, *Constitutionalism and Resistance*, p. 130), and since the Huguenots frequently sought foreign help in this period, Bodin's clear approval of the right of foreign intervention was bold. In the *Apologie de Rene Herpin pour la Republique de I. Bodin*, written by Bodin himself and appended to the 1583 edition of the *République*, he flatly denies that he was intending to invite foreigners into France, but he repeats the general principle in much the same terms (p. 5). There is no particular reason to believe that there was anything disingenuous in this. Bodin took the law of nature very seriously, and was much concerned for its enforcement so long as it did not permit resistance from below.

by a private individual who has been specifically chosen for that task by God and thereby distinguished from the ordinary subject.[13] This latter category, in which Bodin follows the Calvinists, is not intended as a serious exception. The essential reason for including it is to explain certain Biblical examples.

There was, moreover, one sense in which even an ordinary subject could be permitted to use force without admitting a right of resistance in the sense of revolution. Where a private subject was directly and immediately threatened by severe and irreparable injury, he might be entitled to use force in self-defense. Since the principle of self-defense can be distinguished from the power of correction, it need not imply a right of the general community to intervene in behalf of the victim.[14] That Bodin held some notion of this sort is at least a possibility, although the indications are extremely fleeting.[15]

Bodin, finally, was bound to admit the legitimacy of passive disobedience. It was a right that could hardly be denied, since it followed from the principle of conscience, according to the law of nature, and was axiomatic in the religious tradition. But this admission too was theoretically compatible with absolutism. Although passive disobedience is defiance of the ruler's will, it need not imply a power to correct him. It can be taken as mere obedience to higher law, which Bodin had never thought was subject to the ruler's jurisdiction. What he meant by absolute authority was not that the ruler must always be obeyed, no matter what he ordered, but only that he could not be legitimately resisted.

But since Bodin was very much aware that passive disobedience could also be politically explosive, he sought to give it narrow confines. What alarmed him most of all was defiance of orders by the magistrates, the inevitable tendency of which, he thought, was to sow contempt among ordinary subjects,

---

13 *République*, II, 5, p. 305 (224).
14 Thus, for example, Pufendorf, *Law of Nature*, VII, 8, 5, p. 1109.
15 The right of self-defense was often used in early Lutheran doctrine. The idea seemed particularly promising since it could be related to the rule of Roman law that in extreme cases an individual was entitled to ward off extralegal acts of (ordinary) magistrates. By applying this principle to the supreme magistrate, the Lutheran lawyers had a valuable building block for constructing a general doctrine of resistance to the Emperor. (See Benert, *Inferior Magistrates*, ch. 1.) Bodin is apparently alluding to some aspect of self-defense against supreme magistrates in an offhanded and almost inadvertent way. At the end of the passage distinguishing Calvin's list of exceptions to the rule of non-resistance, Bodin appends the following clause: ' although there is a signal difference between assaulting the honor of one's prince, and offering resistance to tyranny, between killing one's king, and offering opposition to his cruelty ' (*République*, II, 5, p. 306 [225]). Since this parenthetical reference is utterly isolated, I have construed it narrowly as the admission of a very limited right of self-defense on the part of the individual, which does not countenance intervention by the general community. This, as noted above, was to be the position taken by later absolutists. Yet I should point out that even thus qualified, the admission of self-defense is not completely consonant with Bodin's general view. His general position, reminiscent of Calvin's, is that the proper remedy for the persecuted subject where no appeals remain in law is either flight or martyrdom. See, for example, *ibid*. p. 307 (225).

not only for the king's authority but for all authority whatever.[16] He thus maintained that passive disobedience was not legitimate unless there was direct violation of the higher law. There is no basis for defiance simply in the fact that a royal order seems not as just or as useful as it might be.[17]

Indeed, even when defiance is legitimate, the magistrate is counselled to avoid a confrontation if evasion is morally permissible. Firm refusals by the magistrates may deter an errant ruler if he is a man of decent inclinations. But if he is a tyrant bent upon his course, gestures of defiance may serve only to infuriate him further, and cost an upright magistrate his life without advantage to the public.[18]

Bodin, finally, also recommended an institutional device that he thought would diminish confrontations. According to an ordinance of France, a dissenting magistrate was permitted to resign his office without punishment, and this policy Bodin endorsed.[19] The discreet departure of dissenters from their office seemed much less dangerous politically than the kinds of open confrontation that might be provoked if resignation were prohibited. But an indirect exception to this rule, which he endorsed, was another royal ordinance by which the dissenting members of a court were required to go along with the majority even if they wished to leave their offices. In this situation, resignations by dissenting magistrates seemed to set too dangerous an example to the public.[20]

Bodin was thus suspicious of any opposition from below that could lead to outright confrontation.[21] But in forbidding resistance absolutely and in confining passive disobedience, he did not anticipate that limitations of the higher

[16] *Ibid*. III, 4, p. 427 (323–4).
[17] *Ibid*. pp. 416–17 (314–15).
[18] *Ibid*. pp. 421–2 (318–19).
[19] *Ibid*. pp. 419–20 (317), p. 427 (324).
[20] *Ibid*. pp. 418–19 (316–17).
[21] Given this doctrine of resistance, Bodin's behavior from 1589 to 1593 seems curious. At the end of 1588, the Catholic League rebelled against Henry III for his assassination of the Duke of Guise, and in 1589 Bodin – who was then a royal magistrate at Laon – publicly adhered to the League. Later in 1589, after Henry III had himself been assassinated, the League supported the claims of Antoine de Bourbon against those of Henry of Navarre. In 1590 Bodin not only accepted Antoine de Bourbon as the legitimate successor, but held that the Duke of Mayenne, who was then the leader of the League, was next in line. Yet up to then Bodin had held, in effect, that Henry of Navarre was next after Henry III according to the Salic law. See *République*, VI, 5, p. 994 (740). In the Latin edition, published only three years before this crisis, Bodin had been even less cautious. See *De republica*, VI, 5, pp. 1147–8.
I do not believe that Bodin's position as to Henry III is really inconsistent with his doctrine of resistance. He did not justify the act of rebellion. He merely treated it as a *fait accompli* which Henry had brought upon himself. He also added a kind of mystical numerology purporting to show that the Valois line was doomed. Bodin may thus be accused of misinterpreting the facts, but not of violating any of his principles. In any event, he was subject to severe threats and psychological pressure at Laon. See Summerfield Baldwin, 'Jean Bodin and the League', *Catholic Historical Review*, XXIII, 2 (July 1937), pp. 160–84; Chauviré, *Jean Bodin*, pp. 77ff; McRae, *Six Bookes*, Introduction, pp. A11–A12; and Jean Moreau-Reibel, 'Bodin et la Ligue d'après des lettres inédites', *Humanisme et Renaissance*, VI (1935) pp. 422–40. Regarding Henry IV, Bodin is surely less consistent,

law, or even of well-established human law, could be easily subverted by a king's caprice. The very basis of his whole position was the implicit assumption that constitutional restraints and the threat of forcible removal were not required to ensure the rule of law. The basis for his confidence, moreover, was something more than the mere good judgment of the king himself. A headstrong king, he thought, could be partially contained by institutional restraints that stopped short of formal limitations. At various places in his work, he makes it very clear that he wished these restraints to be preserved.

He thus continued to insist on a strong and independent magistracy. According to the principle of absolutism, in any conflict between the ruler and the courts, the latter were obliged to yield. But within this limit, he could still maintain that the courts were inherently entitled to pass preliminary judgment on every royal order and to make protests to the king himself. To this extent at least, the older tradition was continued. There was no instruction of the king, no matter what its form, that could prevent preliminary scrutiny once the order was presented to the courts. It was not to be supposed, in other words, that orders of the king, in conflict with established law, were expressions of his true intent, until such time as they were deliberately reiterated.[22]

There were, of course, political dangers in this principle of which Bodin was cognizant. Preliminary scrutiny could be used by the courts as a means of legal obstruction and might sometimes publicly expose the government to embarrassing questions. Bodin wonders at one point whether, in urgent situations, a magistrate might be bound by a letter specifically commanding him to act forthwith. But after momentary hesitation, he concludes that even in the face of such an order, the magistrate is entitled to inform the prince of unjust legal consequences that he may have overlooked.[23] In all other situations the magistrate is inherently entitled to state his remonstrations twice and even thrice.

Another danger was the all but inevitable occurrence of protracted conflicts between the ruler and the courts. If the courts were inherently entitled to examine the legality of orders with respect to laws as well as fact, they would sometimes be required to assume positions on the justice of an act which they could not easily abandon, even if the king insisted, without a compromise of

---

although even here much of his case depends on mystic numerology, which is on a different level, as it were, than the ordinary reasons used in the *République*. His attitude, generally, is that with the country in upheaval, a new king must be named by God.

The more serious moral issue in Bodin's behavior from 1589 to 1593 is whether he was not too hasty, and too timorous, in concluding that the League had triumphed and that the dynasty was overthrown. In 1589, when Henry III was still alive, and after Henry's death, when Henry of Navarre was still in the field, Bodin's judgments of doom were unheroic. But he was not alone in the embarrassment he must have later felt. Many royalist magistrates were caught in a similar dilemma. On the disorientation and apologies of this group, see Roman Schnur, *Die französischen Juristen im konfessionellen Bürgerkrieg des 16. Jahrhunderts* (Berlin, 1962) pp. 48ff.

22 *République*, III, 4, p. 415 (313–14).   23 *Ibid.* p. 426 (322–3).

conscience. This possibility is confronted by Bodin in a comment on the notation *de expresso mandato*. He interprets the notation as an announcement by the court that an act, imposed against its judgment, will not be scrupulously enforced. In this extreme situation, the king is obviously entitled by his right of majesty to punish a delinquent judge, and it is even suggested that he may, if he wishes, forbid the use of the notation.[24]

But since there were manifest risks in forcing confrontation, Bodin anticipates that a king will usually avoid it. The notation *de expresso mandato*, he notes, was an ingenious formula for saving the conscience of the court without affronting the dignity of kings. Although it was a formula for stating reservations, in form at least it was submissive. And very often it was a convenient expedient of royal policy. A king, for example, could be generous in granting pleas to favorites, secure in the knowledge that the courts would later sabotage them. This, then, would appear to be Bodin's rather idiosyncratic explanation as to why the notation *de expresso mandato* appeared so often on the records of the courts. Although in a certain sense it was defiance of the ruler's will, the kings had usually winked at it.[25]

Short of an outright veto, therefore, the courts had considerable power to resist, and they were institutionally protected in their powers since judges, according to Bodin, were virtually irremovable except for cause. Given his absolutist principles, his version of this guarantee could not be quite as iron-clad as it was in the doctrine of the Huguenots. According to the latter, every public officer, no matter how appointed, held his office of the people rather than the king, which was a derivation of the rule of tenure that Bodin could not accept. But he could distinguish, in more traditional fashion, between a mere commissioner, who held his powers simply as an agent and was liable to be dismissed at any time, from a regular official of the crown whose office was established by a statute. On this distinction the magistrate's tenure during good behavior was protected by the rule of law. To dismiss a regular magistrate, who had properly discharged his duties, was to violate a law without good cause and, therefore, to deprive him of a right. It might be done summarily by special derogation from the law, but it still would not be just. The only proper way to get rid of a dutiful official was to repeal the law on which his office was established.[26]

For all practical purposes, therefore, dismissal was an awkward matter.

---

[24] *Ibid*. pp. 417–18 (315–16).   [25] *Ibid*.

[26] *Ibid*. III, 2, p. 378 (282), 387 (288). In the latter passage the rule that the king never dies serves to guarantee the continuity of tenure for officers. In I, 8, p. 153 (106–7), the bestowal of office is incidentally treated as though it were a contract, which seems to be an aberration from Bodin's general conception, unless perhaps he was thinking of fiefs in that context. In medieval law these were treated separately.

It may also be noted that Bodin's rule on tenure applies not only to magistrates but to all regular officers. The term magistrate is properly restricted to a special class of officers holding powers of command. On this distinction, see III, 3, pp. 393ff (294ff).

Under Bodin's rule, of course, it would be technically legitimate for a king to circumvent the courts by attributing functions to commissioners, and this expedient would have a future. It was a threat, however, of which Bodin seems utterly oblivious. He clearly thought that all of the continuing business of the state would be carried on by independent magistrates.

Another expectation was the hope and belief that the kings of France would continue to respect the tradition of public consultation, and that large assemblies might even be convoked more frequently. For Bodin, of course, this obligation was of courtesy rather than necessity. But he could hardly believe that any king of average intelligence and moral decency could wish to govern without good advice.

The one peculiar feature of Bodin's position on advice is his narrow view of the role of the sovereign courts, which was an understandable reaction to the central position of the Parlements in the constitutionalist tradition. As a general rule, he thought, it was extremely dangerous in any state for high judicial powers to be combined in a single body with high functions of political advice, since a body in possession of both functions would all too easily eclipse the sovereign as the focus of political allegiance. In republics this risk is often unavoidable. Since the sovereign is not in continuous assembly, the senate, or the council, must be given administrative powers along with its functions of advice. But one of the great advantages of monarchy is the possibility of allocating these two functions to separate bodies coordinated by the sovereign alone, and it was, according to Bodin, a rule of public policy that the French had long observed. The Parlement of Paris was no longer the senate of the realm – except by honorific title; and its right of remonstration was different from the right of giving counsel. The functions of advice for intimate political affairs were properly restricted to the privy council.

But these objections to political consultation of the sovereign courts did not apply to the Estates, and here Bodin gave full expression to his belief that consultation was desirable. In holding that an Estates assembly was not required for conduct of the government, he did not intend to cast doubt on the political utility of frequent consultations. Large assemblies are recommended to the ruler as the surest way to discover grievances of subjects that might otherwise fester and produce rebellion; they are also recommended as the most convenient way of exposing misconduct by his officers, who might otherwise escape control. The idea that an Estates assembly was a source of strength to kings was commonplace in writings of the time, and one of the favorite models for statements of this theme was a celebrated passage from Philippe de Comines, which Bodin acknowledges and paraphrases: [27]

Nevertheless, just kingship has no foundation more solid than the Estates of the people, and the guilds and corporations. For if the need should arise to raise

[27] *Mémoires*, v, 19.

revenues, assemble forces, and maintain the state against its enemies, this can only be accomplished by the Estates of the people [as a whole], and of every province, town, and community. Thus one sees that even those who would have the Estates of the subjects abolished have no other recourse in their time of need than the Estates and communities which, being brought together, mutually work for the defense and protection of their princes. This is especially true of the general Estates of all the subjects when the prince is present. There, matters of concern to the entire body of the commonwealth and of its members are discussed; there, the just complaints and grievances of poor subjects are heard and recognized; uncovered, there, are all the thefts, frauds, and robberies that have been committed in the name of princes who were unaware of them. But it is unbelievable how reassured the subjects are to see the king preside in their Estates, and how proud they are to be seen by him. If he hears their complaints and receives their petitions, then, even if they are very often disappointed, they still have the glorious feeling of having had access to their prince. This practice is better observed in Spain than in any country in the world, for the Estates used to be assembled there two or three times a year; and in England also because the people grant no taxes if the Estates are not assembled. Yet there are some among us who have tried every means to turn the regional Estates . . . into [royal] elections, claiming that the Estates are nothing but a mob of people. But they deserve the reply that was made by Philippe de Comines to those who said that it was the crime of treason to assemble the Estates.[28]

For Bodin, therefore, the Estates are a desirable and even indispensable institution. So long as it is understood that they do not have to be assembled in order for the king to act, and that there is no obligation on the king to give a satisfactory reply to their petitions, there is no reason for a king to overlook them, and he does so only at his peril.

[28] *République*, III, 7, 500–1 (384–5). See also 1, 8, pp. 141–2 (98).

CHAPTER 7

Concluding Observations

Bodin evidently thought that his later theory of sovereignty was but a clarification of the French tradition and basically consistent with his views in the *Methodus*. In maintaining that the king of France was absolute, he had not intended to discredit all acknowledged limitations, and those that seemed of greatest value he had attempted to incorporate either as derivations from the law of nature or as rules of fundamental law.[1] Accused by a Genevan critic of having given powers to the king that more befitted the subject of a despot than a citizen and member of a commonwealth, Bodin replied with indignation:

I am amazed by those who believe that I have given more power to one man than is becoming to an honest citizen. For specifically in Book I, chapter 8 of my *République* and in other passages as well, I did not hesitate, even in these dangerous times, to refute the opinions of those who would expand the right of the treasury and the regalian prerogatives, and to have taken the ground that these opinions gave kings unlimited power above the law of God and nature. And what could be more public [-spirited] than what I have dared to write – that even kings are not allowed to levy taxes without the fullest consent of the citizens? Or of what importance is it, that I also held that princes are more strictly bound by divine and natural law than those who are subject to their rule? Or that they are obligated by their contracts just as every other citizen? Yet the opposite of this has been taught by almost all the masters of juristic science.[2]

The *République*, however, was more radical than Bodin knew. Almost all the institutional restraints, on which the older writers had tended to insist, were now deprived of binding status. Consent to legislation, by the Parlements or the Estates, was no longer constitutionally required. The review of orders by the courts was reduced to a suspensive check. On many questions the change was subtle and elusive, since the older tradition was ambiguous. But the *République* was radical precisely in the sense that elements of ambiguity that could favor constitutionalist contentions were definitively stripped away.

The importance of this change lies not so much in Bodin's own expectations as to how the government would operate in practice, for on this he was gener-

---

[1] On the correlation of this approach to limitations with Bodin's more appreciative judgment of medieval legal thought at the time the *République* was written, see Ralph E. Giesey, ' The Two Laws in Bodin's Concept of Sovereignty ', paper delivered at *Internationale Bodin Tagung* (Munich, 1970).

[2] *République*, dedicatory letter (originally added to third edition of 1578). A few pages later Bodin cites his opposition at Blois, in which, he says, he risked his life.

ally conventional. The larger significance is the implication of the legal norm itself. The older doctrine tended toward constitutional monarchy. With Bodin, however, a legal path was opened to autocracy. The king was clearly authorized to make important legislative changes without consulting the Estates; he could circumvent the courts and the regular officials of the crown by relying on commissioners. Consent to new taxation, which was the one important barrier that Bodin attempted to make binding, was clearly inconsistent with his basic doctrine and was quickly abandoned by those who succeeded to his general position.

I have tried to show, in chapter 4, that on grounds of accuracy at least, the constitutional doctrine of the *République* held no intellectual advantage over the tradition it tended to replace. The real merit of Bodin's approach, as compared with Pasquier's or Seyssel's, was the greater clarity of his concept of supreme authority, and his use of that concept systematically. But in this respect Bodin's position on the locus of supremacy must be compared to that of the Huguenots, whose theory of sovereignty was also fairly clear, and it is difficult to say that Bodin's findings were more accurate.

Although neither of these latter two conceptions were fully adequate to the delicate balance of the French constitutional tradition, there was a flexibility in the Huguenot approach which its authors had deliberately built in. Their principle of popular sovereignty was qualified by an historical contract between the people and the king, the terms of which could change by mutual agreement. In this fashion they could explain the royal institutions of a later day as the outcome of successive delegations, which were accomplished either by express consent or else by gradual changes in accepted custom. Even this procedure could not do justice to the many subtleties of practice that defied exact analysis in terms of a theory of popular supremacy. The rights of the community were inevitably overstated, those of the king inevitably slighted. There was thus a 'republican' component in the thinking of the Huguenots that Barclay was to identify correctly, if extravagantly, by referring to these writers as monarchomachs.

Yet compared with Bodin's position, the Huguenot solution was somewhat more adaptable to fact. On Bodin's principles no delegation of sovereign authority could have any element of permanence. When he said that the form of government, or the social principle on which offices and honors were distributed, may vary from the form of state, he was not suggesting a constitutional distribution of authority. An absolute king could distribute the right of exercising his power either democratically or aristocratically, or, most preferably, on some combination of these principles.[3] But since Bodin insisted that all engage-

---

[3] *Ibid.* II, 2, pp. 272–3 (200–1), VI, 6, pp. 1050ff (785ff). This distinction between state and government was sometimes confused, in early comments upon Bodin, with division of sovereign authority. An apparent example is Keckermann, *Systema disciplinae politicae*, p. 560.

ments were invalid if their effect was to diminish majesty, no such distribution could be guaranteed by contract, and it could impose no obligation whatsoever beyond the lifetime of any one incumbent. Above all, a king could never be presumed to have undertaken an engagement to abide by decisions of his agents. The elements of consent in the French tradition could not therefore be grounded constitutionally.

If, therefore, one had to choose between these two competing theories of sovereignty in terms of their descriptive possibilities, at least some advantage would have to be given to the Huguenots and to those among the later Catholic League who were to take over and modify their doctrine.

Of the three main alternatives that competed for acceptance in the 1570s, therefore, Bodin's position was perhaps the least successful by empirical criteria. But it was the one that was destined to prevail. The sheer intensity of ideological conflict in this period doomed the older tradition as a means of settling constitutional disputes. It had been supposed in this tradition that the king would always yield to reasonable protests, and that all disagreements could be settled without appeal to some ultimate locus of authority. But in the conflicts of the 1570s, claims of ultimate authority had been seriously advanced, and once the lines of thought represented by Hotman and Bodin had been clearly stated and widely entertained, the question could no longer be suppressed. One sign of this altered situation was the natural movement of all the more significant constitutional disputes of the seventeenth and eighteenth centuries. Those who would oppose the king in the name of traditional practice were very often led to positions reminiscent of the *Francogallia* or would find such views among their followers.

This is not to say that the older tradition simply disappeared. For many Parlementaires and for connoisseurs of the French historical tradition, it was still the best device for understanding institutional relationships. Indeed, from a sociological standpoint it had no rival as a means of understanding the balance of forces on which the survival of the monarchy depended. The Seysselian tradition thus continued to find adherents up through Montesquieu,[4] and through him to leave a permanent impress on the French tradition of legal and political sociology. Irretrievably lost, however, was its broad ideological appeal. It could no longer be used to rally political opinion and to ward off the constitutional crisis that constantly impended in the Old Regime.

The field, accordingly, was left to the lines proceeding from Hotman and Bodin. But of these two tendencies, the first was quickly driven underground. Despite its flamboyant appeal in the 1570s and 1580s, no important segment of opinion was willing to carry on the fight. During the last third of the sixteenth

---

4 For a survey of the development of this and other strands in the first half of the eighteenth century, see Franklin L. Ford, *Robe and Sword* (Cambridge, Mass., 1953; reprinted New York, 1965), ch. 12.

century, many of the leading elements in French society had temporarily inclined to a parliamentary solution of their problems, in large measure because the social risks and dangers in this course had been momentarily obscured by their preoccupation with religious controversies. But at bottom the main components of the French establishment were too divided on the larger social questions, and too attached to the existing scheme of privilege, to sustain their opposition once this preoccupation was removed.

With the religious settlement of the 1590s, the constitutionalist agitation gradually subsided. But its ideological challenge could not be simply forgotten and the older view of limited monarchy restored. The dominant strata, which were to rally to Henry IV, were too weary of the civil wars, too fearful of the popular upheavals which their own opposition had encouraged, and too immediately threatened by the advanced disintegration of the French administration, to look with favor on any questioning of monarchical authority. They were more inclined to some justification of political passivity, which Bodin's doctrine conveniently provided. It clearly and thoroughly repudiated every known legitimation of forcible resistance or constitutionalist challenge from below. Yet at the same time it gave reassurance to established interests by its insistence on the rights of property, on the sanctity of public engagements, and on the general importance of respecting legal continuity. There was even some recognition given to the familiar forms of consultation on what seemed to be a harmless basis.

With opposition dampened, the kings were increasingly able to assert the prerogatives Bodin's theory accorded them.[5] The government, long wary of permitting large assemblies, was fully confirmed in this opinion by what had happened in the various assemblies convoked since 1560. Although the Estates could be dangerous politically, they were ever less disposed to offer subsidies, and the policy of not convening them was to become fundamental for the Bourbon dynasty, which carried on its rule without this form of consent. At the same time, in their efforts to expedite administration, the Bourbons exploited and elaborated all the devices for circumventing the traditional magistracies on matters considered to be highly sensitive. The old administration was thus increasingly overlaid by more bureaucratic and dependent instruments. Bodin was thus deceived in many of his expectations as to how the government would operate. But in law at least his absolutist principle would roughly correspond to the status of the Bourbon kings.

With various refinements and corrections, the absolutism stemming from Bodin was to become the official constitutional doctrine of the Old Regime. His influence, however, was not confined to France, for the *République* was

[5] On the extent to which Bodin's ideas directly influenced the policies and practices of Henry IV and his government, see Ernst Hinrichs, *Fürstenlehre und politisches Handeln im Frankreich Heinrichs IV*, Veröffentlichungen des Max-Planck-Instituts für Geschichte, no. 21 (Göttingen, 1969) especially Part I.

to be esteemed all over Europe as an encyclopedic synthesis of public law and policy.[6] The impact of its constitutional theory was most marked in England and Germany.

In the constitutional conflicts of the seventeenth century, Bodin was to provide the English royalists with a ready-made arsenal of arguments, or, more precisely, with a model for developing their arguments. The *République* would help to show how all medieval checks on royal power could be deprived of binding force – how review by the courts could be reinterpreted as a mere administrative function, how the work of Parliament could be understood as purely advisory or, at the most corroborative, and how all charters and engagements by the king could be construed as conditional and temporary. *Mutatis mutandis*, Bodin's recipe, devised primarily for France, could be applied to England also, and a version of English history developed which somehow found further confirmation through Bodin's thoughts on the indivisibility of sovereignty. Since absolute authority was the natural condition of a proper monarchy, and a ruler who was less than absolute was not a king at all, absolutist theorists like Filmer could readily label their opponents as republicans and anarchists.

In German thought, Bodin's influence on later controversies was even more immediate. His demeaning description of the status of the German Emperor was a challenge to his German readers, and the controversy thus engendered was to guarantee that his theory of sovereignty would become a basic frame of reference for German discussions of the nature of the Empire.[7] But the multiple changes on this theme that were actually devised do not concern us here.

Of much greater interest for present purposes is the rationalization of Bodin's absolutism by legal philosophers like Grotius and Pufendorf, whose concern with the theory of absolutism was less intensely ideological than it was for the English and the French. The purpose of the continental writers was to establish a general legal rationale for European institutions as they actually existed. No attempt was made to show that any particular monarchy was absolute. The fact of absolutism, especially in France, was simply taken as a datum, and the constitutional law of France, more or less in Bodin's version, was implicitly accepted as the norm to which the great majority of kingships tended. The problem, therefore, was to show that absolute authority is consistent with the law of nature, that people may bestow it on a ruler through a contract, that it is the form of state which best fulfills the goal of physical security without denying individual rights.

---

[6] On his reception in England, see Salmon, *The French Religious Wars in English Political Thought, passim.*

[7] On the main responses to and variations of Bodin's account of sovereignty in Germany, see Rudolf Hoke, ' Bodins Einfluss auf die Anfänge der Dogmatik des deutschen Reichsstaatsrechte ', paper delivered at *Internationale Bodin Tagung* (Munich, 1970).

In this process Bodin's idea of absolutism was further refined and qualified and made even more acceptable to moderate opinion. The fundamental laws attaching to the crown were now grounded on an underlying contract. The limitations of the law of nature were now more ingeniously developed. Even the principle of non-resistance was qualified in some respects in order to relieve its grimness.

Yet the dogmatic component still remained. Grotius and Pufendorf, in their own way, were no less cavalier than Barclay or Filmer in their treatment of historical precedent. If the latter two struggled to exorcise the evidence by obscurantist constructions of its meaning, the former sublimely passed it over. In this, they were technically within their rights, for they presented the political contract of absolute subjection as merely one among several formal possibilities that a people might legitimately adopt. Yet they nevertheless managed to insinuate that absolute subjection not only could occur, but had occurred in the majority of kingships. Since neither writer assumed the burden of a proof, they continued, in more subtle form, a dogmatic tendency already encountered in Bodin and endemic in the general position.

For the most part, the history of Bodin's theory of absolutism is a rather dreary tale. The idea was not only a failure ideologically in the sense that different values have prevailed, but its ideological failure was an indication of intrinsic intellectual deficiencies. Despite all the ingenuity expended on it, the more the doctrine was perfected the more it was driven by its inner logic to ignore and banish, as it were, the preceding history of European institutions and the political expectations attending that development. The constitutionalist doctrines of the sixteenth century were the more accurate statement of these facts.

There is, however, a more positive and enduring contribution stemming from Bodin which provides a more cheerful note on which to close. The absolutist trend was soon to become dominant in fact, and, taken as an anticipation of that fact, Bodin's political theory was an appropriate and civilized adjustment. Its emphasis on limitations pointed to the deeper stratum of rights and due procedures on which the absolute monarchy was overlaid. That emphasis was usually preserved in later absolutists, and even developed further by the German theorists.

Bodin's most enduring contribution, furthermore, was more methodological than substantive. The *République* was the partial fulfillment of a vast design for a comprehensive and universal jurisprudence, which was to emancipate the jurist from close dependence on the Roman legal sources. The aim and the effect was not so much to repudiate the principles of Roman law as to widen the sources and the kinds of evidence from which a rationale, and sometimes a critique, could be constructed. When one moves from the commentaries, or even the *consilia*, of a Bartolus or a Baldus to the work of a Grotius, one is struck less by the change of legal rules than by the deeper and more elaborate justification of these rules, by the substitution of historical and political reflections for dogmatic exegesis. The *République*, as I have argued elsewhere, is one important transition from the older to the newer method.[8] Much of the freedom exercised by later writers is already encountered in Bodin, and Grotius himself acknowledges his debt.

The credit for this change is not, of course, Bodin's alone. The idea of a comparative jurisprudence was endemic in his time, and much is owed to Hotman and the Huguenots as well, since their approach was comparative as well as historical. In one respect, indeed, the Huguenots were even more important, since they were among the more immediate sources for the contractual idea on which the later theory of public law was founded. The result was a strange but methodologically happy marriage between the intellectual descendants of Hotman and Bodin. In constitutionalist writers like Althusius, Bodin's terminology of public law is often used to express a political doctrine reminiscent of the *Vindiciae contra tyrannos* and often drawn from it directly. In Grotius and Pufendorf, the idea of an original contract, which in large part is borrowed indirectly from the Huguenots, is used to give a deeper base to Bodin's absolutism.

But even on the substantive level, Bodin's more enduring contribution is significant if indirect. His theory of sovereignty was the proximate source of the idea that there must exist in every legal system an ultimate legal norm or set of procedures by which all decisions are coordinated. Put in older language, a sovereign power must exist in every commonwealth, and must always be located in the norms accepted by the general community. Bodin wrongly thought that this authority must be vested in what we would call the government. But it is with Bodin's work that discussion of this issue was effectively initiated.

Bodin, finally, was among the very first to discuss the classification of governmental powers from a modern point of view, and to indicate the relationships among them. His idea of the priority of legislative power and the subordination of all others to this first portended a fundamental revolution in the analysis and classification of governmental forms. Here again Bodin was often wrong, not only in his results but in his rationale. Yet here too he is the source of a continuing tradition. In most areas of public law, Bodin's bold efforts to clarify the meaning and content of sovereignty, and to construct a legal conception of the state that could be universally applied, were a fundamental starting point for modern thought.

---

[8] Franklin, *Jean Bodin and the Methodology of Law and History*.

Perpetuity as a Criterion of Sovereign Status

In Book I, chapter 8 of the *République* sovereign power is defined as perpetual as well as absolute.[1] Since the issue of perpetuity had practically no importance in the constitutional controversies of the time, and since it is only loosely related to other elements in Bodin's doctrine, there was no convenient place to introduce it in the text. There are, however, one or two interesting technical questions posed by the test of perpetuity, which would seem to justify a brief appendix.

By perpetuity of power, as applied to a monarchical state, Bodin meant tenure for life. An elective ruler, as well as an hereditary ruler, could therefore be a proper sovereign as long as his authority was absolute. But even where a magistrate held absolute authority, he did not have the status of a sovereign if his tenure of power was fixed by a definite limit (which might conceivably fall within his lifetime), or if his tenure of power was precarious and could be revoked at the discretion of another. An approximate example of the first limitation was the position of the Roman dictator. At least in the classical republic, he held virtually absolute authority for an outer limit of six months. A good example of the second was the position of lieutenant-general sometimes created by the kings of France. Although its powers were extremely large, it could be revoked at the pleasure of the king.[2]

The interesting questions arise from the first of these two cases. Bodin's denial of sovereign status to an absolute authority holding power for a definite term is a dubious proposition, and it was considered highly debatable by later writers.[3]

The evident basis of Bodin's position is the idea that a sovereign authority must not be subject to any condition whatsoever. Where absolute authority is limited in time, a condition obviously exists. The power must be surrendered at a given date. If it is extended beyond that date without consent, the holder is a mere usurper and becomes exposed to legitimate resistance. This cannot happen with an hereditary ruler or an elective king for life.

On the other hand, the tenure of absolute authority held for a fixed term is obviously not conditional at any point within that term. This would not apply, of course, if the tenure were precarious. But even in this latter case the problem is not

---

[1] *République*, 1, 8, p. 122 (84). In the Latin edition the attribute of perpetuity is not included in this opening definition. But this is not significant. The criterion of perpetuity appears in both editions in a restatement of the definition a few pages later. In both editions, furthermore, the mode of treatment is the same. The examination of sovereign authority begins with the meaning of ' perpetual ' and then goes on to ' absolute '. See E. Hancke, *Bodin, eine Studie über der Begriff der Souveränität* (Breslau, 1894; reprinted by Scientia Verlag, Aalen, Germany, 1969) p. 8.

[2] *République*, 1, 8, pp. 122-8 (84-8).

[3] See Grotius, *Law of War and Peace*, 1, 3, 11, pp. 113-15; Pufendorf, *Law of Nature*, VII, 6, 15, pp. 1079-80.

the existence of limitation as to time. It is rather that the authority bestowed is less than absolute because the donor of the power remains continuously active and empowered. But where the term of authority is fixed, the donor of absolute authority is temporarily deprived of any right of recovery or opposition. There is thus no better reason to deny the status of a sovereign to a holder of absolute authority because there is a definite limit to his term, than to deny that status to an elective or successive monarch because he cannot name his own successor.

In strict logic, therefore, we should probably criticize Bodin for having insisted upon perpetuity. But from a common-sense perspective his position has a certain merit. In most cases the creation of temporary absolute authority is a provisional departure from the normal form of state. One might imagine an elective, or perhaps even an hereditary, monarchy, with constitutional provision for mandatory retirement – let us say, at the age of 65. But this would be an idle fantasy. The usual situation is an emergency office like the Roman dictatorship or a kind of emergency commission of the sort that was held by the Decemviri.[4] In all such cases the very office is intended to be temporary, and it thus sounds slightly odd to speak of its holder as ' the ' sovereign.[5]

[4] But Pufendorf, *Law of Nature*, vii, 6, 15, p. 1079, gives one example that clearly goes further. Michael Paleologus of Byzantium swore to resign his throne as soon as his son and heir should come of age. The oath, notes Pufendorf, was never kept.

[5] In most cases, furthermore, the appointment would carry some express or implicit charge, or the holder would be denied the name of king or other title suggesting majesty. In discussing the question, Bodin maintains that where a charge is attached or where the title is withheld, sovereign power is reserved by the donor. For this reason, his discussion of particular cases is uncertain. It is not fully clear on what grounds he would deny sovereign status. Questions of charge and title also explain certain disagreements on specific cases between Grotius and Pufendorf. The latter is more cautious in extending the status of sovereign.

On the Question of Earlier Sources for Bodin's Idea of Indivisibility

I feel fairly sure that Bodin's idea of indivisibility was not influenced by the thought of any earlier writer. Some elaboration is required to clarify this judgment. But since my findings on influence are negative, I decided not to discuss them in the text or in a lengthy footnote.

In one passage Bodin almost casually remarks that his idea of indivisibility had some connection with the well-known rule of medieval civil law forbidding the ruler to alienate his power.[1] But if there is a connection, it is vague and loose, and seems to depend more on certain verbal similarities than on any basic similarity of principles.

I am aware of two statements in the civilian literature that Bodin probably knew and could have had in mind. One of these occurs in a lengthy comment by Chasseneuz designed to show that a ruler may not concede, or alienate, the insignia of his office. Among many other arguments, Chasseneuz includes the following:

> Just as the prince may not alter the character of his office (*dignitatem suam immutare*), so, by analogy, neither may he concede the insignia of that office to another; because by that act there would be two heads in a single body, which would be monstrous.[2]

One can well understand how Bodin could have looked upon this language, or similar language in some other source, as authority for his views on indivisibility. Yet Chasseneuz is simply saying that a prince cannot retain sovereignty and yet concede it to another, without producing a juridical absurdity. He does not hold, either expressly or by implication, that a mixed constitution is impossible.

The other passage is from Baldus and seems to deal, not with the sharing or functional distribution of authority, but with the question of territorial integrity. This, it may be noted, was the usual bearing of the rule against alienation, which forbade the ruler to cede any part of his domain to the control of a subject or a foreigner. In this sense, furthermore, the legal objection was not derived from any logical absurdity in division, but was normally grounded on a positive rule of fundamental law, like the *lex regia* of civil law.

Baldus might seem to be holding something more, since he says that *imperium est indivisibile*. But this phraseology is highly exceptional in medieval civil law, and the rest of the passage, as well as the context in which it occurs, strongly

---

[1] *République*, I, 10, p. 215 (155) quoted above, p. 59.
[2] Chasseneuz, *Catalogus*, p. 32.

indicates that the underlying thought is quite conventional.[3] Baldus seems simply to be saying that the obligation of a prince to maintain his realm intact is natural as well as positive. A prince who gave away a portion of his kingdom would do violence to the moral goal of human unity, and perhaps also to the metaphysical principle that division of existing unities is bad. What Bodin has in common with Baldus and other medievals is a deep objection to excessive fragmentation. But I find nothing in the medieval civil law tradition that specifically anticipates Bodin's juridical objections to the sharing of governmental powers.

More closely related is an argument on church organization by the Dominican theologian, Juan de Torquemada. Torquemada was a papal absolutist, and in one part of his *summa de ecclesia* of 1449 he engages in a massive polemic against the conciliarist theses put forward at the Councils of Constance and Basel. At one point in his lengthy list of arguments, he attempts to show a contradiction in the conciliarist position. It had been admitted at the Council of Constance that there was a sense in which the Pope could be regarded as supreme even though the *plenitudo potestatis* of the Church was ultimately vested in the entire body of the faithful. According to Torquemada this dual supremacy could mean only one of two things. Either the supremacy vested in the Church and the supremacy vested in the Pope are two distinct absolute supremacies (fullnesses of power) differing only in number. Or else the Church and the Pope are in possession of (share?) one and the same fullness of power. But on the first hypothesis there would be two absolute supremacies in one association, which is clearly an absurdity; and on the second hypothesis the Church would have no government at all, since the Church could not command the Pope, and the Pope could not command the Church.[4]

Torquemada's criticism of the first hypothesis is not of interest for present purposes. But his objections to the second, if I have interpreted that hypothesis correctly, would clearly anticipate the line of reasoning followed by Bodin in his holding that sovereignty cannot be shared.

---

[3] The statement appears in a comment on the *Proemium* to the *Digest* (Baldus, *Super Prima Digesti Veteris*, Lyon, 1535, f. 2v). The prince, he argues, ' cannot diminish the rights of majesty (*jura imperii*) and give away one part while holding on to another. Majesty (*imperium*) is indivisible and an indivisible entity attracts to itself what is not an entity . . . Furthermore, it [majesty] is corrupted by a change in form because it is something to be ruled by one . . . and because by the same reasoning [that would justify a first donation], other emperors could give away now one province, now another, and the entire majesty (*imperium*) would be annihilated . . .'

[4] Juan de Torquemada, *Summa de ecclesia* (1449) (Venice, 1561) II, 71, p. 198. The argument is reproduced in part in an appendix of excerpts from Torquemada's Latin in Antony Black, *Monarchy and Community* (Cambridge, 1970) p. 170. The following is from Black's translation at p. 74: ' The fullness of power which is located in the church is either one and the same in identity (*numero*) with that which is located in the pope, or it is different. But it cannot be said that it is different, because then there would be two supreme powers, or fullnesses of power, which cannot be . . . This fullness of power cannot be said to be one and the same in identity, because in that case neither would the pope be superior and prelate, nor could it be said that the church was superior in power to the Roman bishop himself . . . because if " equal cannot command equal ", far less can it do so when there is identity (*identitas*) of power.'

I am indebted to Mr Andrew Lynch, who is a member of my graduate colloquium at Columbia University, for calling my attention to this passage.

There is no indication, however, that Bodin was familiar with Torquemada's work or had any interest in the debates of the conciliar and later conciliar epoch. In any event, the argument from indivisibility is not very central in the *Summa de ecclesia* and seems not to have been widespread at the time. It is not very likely, furthermore, that Bodin would have come across echoes of the argument in the writings of contemporary theologians or canonists. Some, although not all, of the papalists in Bodin's period make use of the argument that two supreme authorities cannot exist within a single body, in which they are perhaps reproducing Torquemada.[5] But the second part of Torquemada's argument – which is more obscure and was less immediately useful to the papalists – seems to have been passed over and forgotten.[6]

[5] This part of the argument does appear in Thomas Cajetan (Tommaso de Vio Gaetani), *De auctoritate Papae et Concilii* (1511) in Juan Tomas Rocaberti de Perelada, ed., *Bibliotheca maxima pontificia* (Rome, 1697–9) vol. xix (pp. 463–561), 1, 7, p. 455. But I do not find it in Thomas Campeggi, *De auctoritate et potestate Pontificis Romani in Ecclesia Dei* in Rocaberti, xix (pp. 568–618) even though Campeggi's long list of arguments seems to be intended as a compendium. It may also be noted that Bodin acknowledges no intellectual debt to Cajetan although in one or two places of the *République* he reports the latter's activities as Cardinal and papal legate. In any event, the thought that there cannot be two supreme powers in a single body was not very novel.

[6] For a general account of Torquemada's political ideas, see Black, *Monarchy and Community*, pp. 53–80.

Bibliography

SOURCES

Andrea Alciato, *Paradoxa* in Andrea Alciato, *Opera*, Basel, 1582, vol. IV.

Johannes Althusius, *Politica methodice digesta*, Cambridge (Mass.), 1932.

Henning Arnisaeus, *Doctrina politica in genuinam methodum quae est Aristotelis reducta* in Henning Arnisaeus, *Opera politica omnia*, Strasbourg, 1648.

Baldus de Ubaldis, *Consilia sive responsa*, 3 vols, Venice, 1575, vols I, III, IV.

Praelectiones in Codicem, 4 vols, Lyon, 1556, vol. I.

Super Prima Digesti Veteris, Lyon, 1535.

Bartolus de Saxoferrato, *Commentarii*, 11 vols, Venice, 1590, vols I, V, VII.

François Baudouin, *De institutione historiae universae et ejus cum jurisprudentia conjunctione* Προλεγόμενων, Halle, 1726.

Pedro Belluga, *Speculum principum ac justitiae*, Paris, 1530.

Guillaume Benoist (Benedictus), *Repetitio in cap. Raynutius, extra testamentis et uxorem nomine Adelasiam*, Lyon, 1583.

Christopher Besold, *De majestate in genere ejusque juribus specialibus ... accedit tractatio singularis de reipublicae statu mixto* in Christopher Besold, *Operis politici, editio nova*, Strasbourg, 1626.

Theodore Beza (de Bèze), *Right of Magistrates* in Julian H. Franklin, ed. and trans., *Constitutionalism and Resistance in the Sixteenth Century*, New York, 1969.

Jean Bodin, *Apologie de Rene Herpin pour la Républicque de I. Bodin* in Jean Bodin, *Six livres de la république*, Paris, 1583; reprinted by Scientia Verlag, Aalen, Germany, 1961.

Colloquium heptaplomeres de rerum sublimium arcanis abditis, L. Noack, ed., Schwerin, 1857.

Juris universi distributio, Pierre Mesnard, ed., *Oeuvres philosophiques de Jean Bodin*, Paris, 1951.

Methodus ad facilem historiarum cognitionem, Pierre Mesnard, ed., *Oeuvres philosophiques de Jean Bodin*, Paris, 1951.

Method for the Easy Comprehension of History, Beatrice Reynolds, trans., New York, 1945.

Recueil de tout ce qui s'est négocié en la compagnie du tiers-état de France en l'assemblée générale des trois états, assigné par le roi en la ville de Blois au 15 novembre 1576 in C.-H. Mayer, *Des Etats généraux et autres assemblées nationales*, Paris and The Hague, 1788, vol. XIII.

Response à M. de Malestroit in Henri Hauser, *La vie chère au XVIᵉ siècle, La response de Jean Bodin à M. de Malestroit*, Paris, 1932.

114

Jean Bodin—*continued*.

Les six livres de la république, Paris, 1583; reprinted by Scientia Verlag, Aalen, Germany, 1961.

The Six Bookes of a Commonweale, facsimile reprint of Knolles translation of 1606 with apparatus and introduction by Kenneth D. McRae, Cambridge (Mass.), 1962.

De republica libri sex, Paris, 1586.

Nicholas Bohier (Boerius, Boyer), *Additiones* to Jean Montaigne, *Tractatus de parlamentis et collatione parlamentorum* in *Tractatus universi juris*, Venice, 1584–6, vol. xvi.

Tractatus de ordine et praecedentia graduum utriusque fori in *Tractatus universi juris*, Venice, 1584–6, vol. xvi.

Guillaume Budé, *Annotationes in quatuor et viginti Pandectarum libros*, Paris, 1535.

Vincent Cabot (Cabotius), *Variarum juris publici et privati disputationum libri duo* in Gerard Meerman, ed., *Novus thesaurus juris civilis et canonici*, The Hague, 1751–3, vol. iv.

Thomas Cajetan (Tommaso de Vio Gaetani), *De auctoritate Papae et Concilli* in Juan Tomas Rocaberti de Perelada, ed., *Bibliotheca maxima pontificia*, Rome, 1697–9, vol. xix.

John Calvin, *Institutes of the Christian Religion*, John Allen, trans., Grand Rapids, 1949.

Thomas Campeggi, *De auctoritate et potestate Pontificis Romani in ecclesia Dei* in Juan Tomas Rocaberti de Perelada, ed., *Bibliotheca maxima pontificia*, Rome, 1697–9, vol. xix.

Barthélemy de Chasseneuz, *Catalogus gloriae mundi*, Geneva, 1649.

Consuetudines Ducatus Burgundiae, Geneva, 1616.

René Choppin, *De domanio Franciae libri tres*, Frankfurt, 1701.

Philippe de Comines, *Mémoires*, J. Calmette and G. Durville, eds., 3 vols, Paris, 1965, vol. ii.

Jacques Cujas, *Observationes et emendationes* in Jacques Cujas, *Opera*, Prato, 1836.

Jean Ferrault, *Tractatus . . . jura seu privilegia aliqua regni Franciae continens* bound together with Charles de Grassaille, *Regalium Franciae libri duo*, Paris, 1545.

Robert Gaguin, *Compendium super Francorum gestis, s, l,* 1511.

Innocent Gentillet, *Anti-Machiavel*, Geneva, 1576; reprinted with notes by C. E. Rathé, Geneva, 1968.

Jean Gillot, *De jurisdictione et imperio* in *Tractatus universi juris*, Venice, 1584–6, vol. iii.

Charles de Grassaille, *Regalium Franciae libri duo*, Paris, 1545.

Peter Gregory (Grégoire) of Toulouse, *De Republica libri sex et viginti*, Frankfurt, 1609.

Hugo Grotius, *On the Law of War and Peace*, F. W. Kelsey trans., Oxford, 1925.

Cosme Guymier, *Pragmatica Sanctio una cum reportorio*, Paris, 1504.

Bernard de Girard (Du Haillan), *De l'estat et succez des affaires de France*, Paris, 1571.

Histoire générale des roys de France, 2 vols, Paris, 1615.

François Hotman, *Antitribonianus* in *Variorum opuscula ad cultiorem jurisprudentiam adsequendam pertinentia*, Pisa, 1771, vol. VII.

Consilia in François Hotman, *Operum tomus primus* (*-tertius*), 3 vols, Geneva, 1599–1600, vol. II.

Francogallia, in Julian H. Franklin, *Constitutionalism and Resistance in the Sixteenth Century*, New York, 1969.

Francogallia, Ralph E. Giesey ed., John H. M. Salmon trans., Cambridge (forthcoming).

Quaestiones illustres in François Hotman, *Operum tomus primus* (*-tertius*), 3 vols, Geneva, 1599–1600, vol. II.

F. A. Isambert, *Recueil général des anciennes lois françaises*, 29 vols, Paris, 1821–33, vols VI, XIV.

Bartholomaeus Keckermann, *Systema disciplinae politicae*, Hanover, 1607.

Charles Loyseau, *Traité des seigneuries* in Charles Loyseau, *Oeuvres*, Lyon, 1701.

Antoine Matharel [with Jean Papire Masson], *Ad F. Hotomani Franco-galliam responsio*, Paris, 1575.

Jason de Maino, *Consilia sive responsa*, Venice, 1581.

In Primam Digesti Veteris Partem commentaria, Venice, 1589.

Philippe de Mornay, *Vindiciae contra tyrannos*, in Julian H. Franklin, *Constitutionalism and Resistance in the Sixteenth Century*, New York, 1969.

Etienne Pasquier, ' De l'authorité royale ' in Dorothy Thickett, ed., *Estienne Pasquier, Écrits politiques*, Geneva, 1966.

Pourparler du prince, Paris, 1560.

Les recherches de la France, Paris, 1607.

Polybius, *Histories*, W. R. Paton trans., Loeb Classical Library, London, 1923.

Samuel Pufendorf, *On the Law of Nature and Nations*, C. H. and W. A. Oldfather trans., Oxford, 1934.

Pierre Rebuffi, *Commentarii in constitutiones seu ordinationes regias*, 3 vols, Lyon, 1554.

Explicatio ad quatuor Pandectarum libros, Lyon, 1589.

Bernard de la Roche-Flavin, *Treze livres des Parlemens de France*, Bordeaux, 1617.

Claude de Seyssel, *La monarchie de France*, Jacques Poujol, ed., Paris, 1961.

Prohème en la translation de l'Histoire d'Appien in Claude de Seyssel, *La Monarchie de France*, Jacques Poujol, ed., Paris, 1961.

Alessandro Tartagni (Alexander Imolensis), *Consilia*, 3 vols, Venice, 1597, vol. II.

Juan de Torquemada (Turrecremata), *Summa de ecclesia*, Venice, 1561.

Nicholas Tudeschis (Panormitanus), *Super Tertio Decretalium*, Lyon, 1559.

Fernando Vazquez de Menchaca (Vasquius), *Controversiarum illustrium . . . libri tres*, 3 vols, Valladolid, 1931, vol. I.

Ulrich Zasius, *Opera omnia*, Lyon, 1550; reprinted by Scientia Verlag, Aalen, Germany, 7 vols, 1964, vol. I.

Bibliography

SECONDARY WORKS

J. W. Allen, *Political Thought in the Sixteenth Century*, London, 1928; reprinted with bibliographical additions, London, 1957.

E. Armstrong, *The French Wars of Religion : Their Political Aspect*, London, 1904.

Summerfield Baldwin ' Jean Bodin and the League ', *Catholic Historical Review*, vol. XXIII, no. 2, July 1937, pp. 160–84.

C. R. Baxter, ' Jean Bodin's Daemon and His Conversion to Judaism ', paper delivered at *Internationale Bodin Tagung*, Munich, 1970.

Richard R. Benert, ' Inferior Magistrates in Sixteenth-Century Political and Legal Thought ', unpublished doctoral dissertation, University of Minnesota, 1967.

Antony Black, *Monarchy and Community*, Cambridge, 1970.

John L. Brown, *The Methodus ad facilem historiarum cognitionem, A Critical Study*, Washington, D.C., 1939.

Vittorio de Caprariis, *Propaganda e pensiero politico in Francia durante le guerre di religione, I, 1559–1572*, Naples, 1959.

R. W. and A. J. Carlyle, *A History of Medieval Political Theory in the West*, 6 vols, Edinburgh and London, 1909–36, vol. VI.

Roger Chauviré, *Jean Bodin, auteur de la République*, La Flèche, 1914.

William F. Church, *Constitutional Thought in Sixteenth-Century France*, Cambridge (Mass.), 1941; reprinted New York, 1969.

Claude Collot, *L'École doctrinale de droit public de Pont-à-Mousson*, Paris, 1965.

Roger Doucet, *Étude sur le gouvernement de François Ier dans ses rapports avec le Parlement de Paris*, Paris, 1921.

Les institutions politiques de la France au XVIe siècle, Paris, 1948.

Franklin L. Ford, *Robe and Sword*, Cambridge (Mass.), 1953; reprinted New York, 1965.

Julian H. Franklin, *Constitutionalism and Resistance in the Sixteenth Century*, New York, 1969.

' Jean Bodin ', *International Encyclopedia of the Social Sciences*, 17 vols (New York, 1968), vol. II.

' Jean Bodin and the End of Medieval Constitutionalism ', paper delivered at *Internationale Bodin Tagung*, Munich, 1970.

Jean Bodin and the Sixteenth Century Revolution in the Methodology of Law and History, New York, 1963.

Aldo Garosci, *Jean Bodin : politica e diritto nel Rinascimento francese*, Milan, 1934.

Otto von Gierke, *Natural Law and the Theory of Society*, Ernest Barker trans., Cambridge, 1934; reprinted Boston, 1957.

Ralph E. Giesey, *If Not, Not : The Oath of the Aragonese and the Legendary Laws of Sobrarbe*, Princeton, 1968.

The Juristic Basis of Dynastic Right to the French Throne, Philadelphia, 1961.

The Royal Coronation Ceremony in Renaissance France, Geneva, 1960.

' The Two Laws in Bodin's Concept of Sovereignty ', paper delivered at *Internationale Bodin Tagung*, Munich, 1970.

' Why and When Hotman Wrote the *Francogallia* ', *Bibliothèque d'Humanisme et Renaissance*, xxix (1967) pp. 583–611.

ed. and John H. M. Salmon, trans., *Francogallia by François Hotman*, Cambridge (forthcoming).

Myron P. Gilmore, *Argument from Roman Law in Political Thought : 1200–1600*, Cambridge (Mass.), 1941.

' Authority and Property in the Seventeenth Century : The First Edition of the *Traité des seigneuries* of Charles Loyseau ', *Harvard Library Bulletin*, iv (1950), no. 2, pp. 258–65.

E. Hancke, *Bodin, eine Studie über der Begriff der Souveränität*, Breslau, 1894; reprinted by Scientia Verlag, Aalen, Germany, 1969.

Ernst Hinrichs, *Fürstenlehre und politisches Handeln im Frankreich Heinrichs IV*, Veröffentlichungen des Max-Planck-Instituts für Geschichte, no. 21, Göttingen, 1969.

' Das Fürstenbild Bodins und die Krise der französischen Renaissance-monarchie ', paper delivered at *Internationale Bodin Tagung*, Munich, 1970.

Rudolf Hoke, ' Bodins Einfluss auf die Anfänge der Dogmatik des deutschen Reichsstaatsrechte ', paper delivered at *Internationale Bodin Tagung*, Munich, 1970.

Ernst H. Kantorowicz, *The King's Two Bodies*, Princeton, 1957.

Donald R. Kelley, ' The Development and Context of Bodin's Method ', paper delivered at *Internationale Bodin Tagung*, Munich, 1970.

Foundations of Modern Historical Scholarship : Language, Law, and History in the French Renaissance, New York and London, 1970.

Hotman, Princeton (forthcoming).

' Murd'rous Machiavel in France : a Post-Mortem ', *Political Science Quarterly*, lxxxv, no. 4, December 1970, pp. 545–59.

André Lemaire, *Les lois fondamentales de la monarchie française d'après les théoriciens de l'ancien régime*, Paris, 1907.

J. Russell Major, ' The Renaissance Monarchy : A Contribution to the Periodization of History ', *The Emory University Quarterly*, xiii, no. 2, June 1957, pp. 112–24.

Representative Institutions in Renaissance France, 1421–1559, Madison, 1960.

Edouard Maugis, *Histoire du Parlement de Paris de l'avènement des rois Valois à la mort d'Henri IV*, 3 vols, Paris, 1913–16, vol. 1.

Kenneth D. McRae, ' The Political Thought of Jean Bodin ', unpublished doctoral dissertation, Harvard, 1953.

Introduction and notes, *The Six Bookes of a Commonweale by Jean Bodin*, facsimile reprint of Knolles translation of 1606, Cambridge (Mass.), 1962.

Pierre Mesnard, *L'Essor de la philosophie politique au XVIᵉ siècle*, 2nd ed., Paris, 1951.

' La pensée religieuse de Bodin ', *Revue du seizième siècle*, xvi (1929), pp. 71–121.

Jean Moreau-Reibel, ' Bodin et la Ligue d'après des lettres inédites ', *Bibliothèque d'Humanisme et Renaissance*, vi (1935), pp. 422–40.

Jean Bodin et le droit public comparé dans ses rapports avec la philosophie de l'histoire, Paris, 1933.

Roland Mousnier and Fritz Hartung, ' Quelques problèmes concernant la monarchie absolue ', *Relazioni del X congresso internazionale di scienze storiche*, Florence, 1955, IV, *Storia moderna*, pp. 3–55.

Ugo Nicolini, *La proprietá, il principe, e l'espropriazione per publica utilitá*, Milan, 1940.

F. Olivier-Martin, *Histoire du droit français*, Paris, 1948.

Jacques Poujol, ' Jean Ferrault on the King's Privileges: A Study of the Medieval Sources of Renaissance Political Theory in France ', *Studies in the Renaissance*, 5, 1958, pp. 15–26.

Beatrice Reynolds, *Proponents of Limited Monarchy in Sixteenth Century France : Francis Hotman and Jean Bodin*, New York, 1931.

Melvin Richter, ' The History of the Concept of Despotism ', *Dictionary of the History of Ideas*, New York (forthcoming).

Peter N. Riesenberg, *Inalienability of Sovereignty in Medieval Political Thought*, New York, 1956.

Georg Roellenblek, *Offenbarung, Natur, und jüdische Überlieferung bei Jean Bodin*, Kassel, 1964.

' Der Schluss des *Heptaplomeres* und die Begründung der Toleranz bei Bodin ', paper delivered at *Internationale Bodin Tagung*, Munich, 1970.

Lucien Romier, *Le royaume de Catherine de Médicis*, 2 vols, Paris, 1925.

John H. M. Salmon, ' Bodin and the Monarchomachs ', paper delivered at the *Internationale Bodin Tagung*, Munich, 1970.

The French Religious Wars in English Political Thought, Oxford, 1959.

Letter to the editor, *Times Literary Supplement*, 11 December 1969.

See also Giesey.

Roman Schnur, *Die französischen Juristen im konfessionellen Bürgerkrieg des 16. Jahrhunderts*, Berlin, 1962.

Cynthia G. Shoenberger, ' The Confession of Magdeburg and the Lutheran Doctrine of Resistance ', unpublished doctoral dissertation, Columbia, 1972.

Owen Ulph, ' Jean Bodin and the Estates-General of 1576 ', *Journal of Modern History*, XIX, no. 4, December 1947, pp. 289–96.

Georges Weill, *Les théories sur le pouvoir royal en France pendant les guerres de religion*, Paris, 1891.

Martin Wolfe, ' Jean Bodin on Taxes: The Sovereignty-Taxes Paradox ', *Political Science Quarterly*, LXXXIII, no. 2, June 1968, pp. 268–84.

Cecil N. Sidney Woolf, *Bartolus of Sassoferrato*, Cambridge, 1913.

Gaston Zeller, *Les institutions politiques de la France au XVIe siècle*, Paris, 1948.

Index

Index

law, French, 6–10, 12–22, 47
law, fundamental, 102, 107, 111
  see also domain, alienation of; succession,
  law of
law, Roman, 6–10, 12, 14, 16, 23–4, 57, 74n,
  78n, 84, 96n
Lemaire, André, 21n
Le Roy, Louis, 17
lettre de jussion, 18, 19, 21, 22n
Louis XI, King of France, 46
Louis XII, King of France, 2
Loyseau, Charles, 92
Luther, Martin, 43, 44, 94

Machiavelli, N., 49
McRae, Kenneth D., 49n, 50n, 97n
Magdeburg, 44
magistrates, 16, 24–5, 38, 45, 79, 86
  see also resistance
Maguis, Edouard, 5n
Maino, Jason de, 14, 81n
Martel, Charles, 11
Mary Tudor, 65
Matharel, Antoine, 53n, 72n
Mayenne, Duke of, 97n
Mesnard, Pierre, 1n, 25n, 26n, 48n
Metz, Bodin at, 50n
monarchy, 3, 5, 23, 26, 28, 35, 36, 84
  see also kingship
Montaigne, Jean, 8n, 11n
Montesquieu, Baron de, 7, 104
Mousnier, Roland, 1n

nature, law of, 46, 79–81, 84–6, 95n, 106–7
  as binding on royal promises, 37, 54, 55,
  58, 62
Navarre, Henry of, 97n
Nicolini, Ugo, 15n
noblesse de robe, 4

oaths, 37–8, 54–62, 82
  see also promises
offices, sale of, 5, 47

Paleologus, Michael, 110n
Papinian, 64
Parlement of Paris, 3–5, 7–10, 16, 18, 45, 100
  as French version of early Roman Senate,
  7–9
  Bodin on, 66–7
  du Haillan on, 20
  historical origins of, 11, 12
  power of ratification and, 10, 11
Parlements, 20, 21, 45, 65, 69, 83
  see also constitutionalism; Parlement of
  Paris
Parliament, English, *see* consent; taxation

Pasquier, Etienne, 18, 19–20
perpetuity, 109–10
Persians, 36
Philip the Fair, 20, 76
Placentinus, 15n
plenitudo potestatis, 12–16, 18n
Poland, king of, 39, 49n, 68–9
Polybius, 31, 32
Pot, Philip, 73n
Poujol, Jacques, 7n
prerogatives, 24, 25, 26, 30, 39, 57
privileges, 2, 7n, 13n, 15, 24, 25, 68n
promises, 17–18, 45, 60n, 62, 68n
  see also oaths
property, rights of, 1n, 79, 85, 105
Pufendorf, Samuel, 34n, 78n, 106, 107, 110n

Rebuffi, Pierre, 16, 19n
religious toleration, 41–2, 48
remonstration, right of, 5, 19, 21, 22n, 66–9,
  100
Renaissance, 3, 4
rescripts, 9, 12, 13n, 15, 38
resistance, 93–101
  Bodin on, 50–2, 62, 67
  courts and, 5, 12, 15, 98–100
  Estates and, 46, 93–5
  Huguenot theory of, 42, 43–4, 46–7
  legitimate, 43, 50–2, 71
  Luther and Calvin on, 43–4, 94, 96n
  magistrates and, 43–4, 46, 93, 94, 96–9
  passive disobedience, 96–7
Richter, Melvin, 84n
Riesenberg, Peter N., 24n, 76n
Roche, Bernard de la, 19
Roellenblek, Georg, 48n
Romier, Lucien, 2n
Romulus, 7
royal obligation, 58, 79–84, 85–6
  see also oaths
royal patronage, 2, 3
royal power, 2, 14, 16–17, 23–4, 28, 31

St Bartholomew's Day Massacre, 1, 41, 43, 44,
  49
Salic law, 45, 71–2, 76, 77
Salmon, J. H. M., 44n
Scythians, 37
Senate, Roman, 7–10, 32, 33, 64
Seneca, 84
Seyssel, Claude de, 14, 15, 17, 18, 34, 40, 70n,
  104
sovereignty, 23–40, 50–1, 53n, 57, 68, 93–4
  inalienability of, 23–4, 28, 61n, 111–12
  indivisibility of, 23, 26–9, 31, 68
  rights of, 32
  see also constitution, mixed; supremacy

123